Maxine Hong Kingston

MANCHESTER
1824

Manchester University Press

Contemporary World Writers

SERIES EDITOR   JOHN THIEME

Maxine Hong Kingston

HELENA GRICE

Manchester University Press
Manchester and New York

distributed exclusively in the USA by Palgrave

Published by Manchester University Press
Oxford Road, Manchester M13 9NR, UK
and Room 400, 175 Fifth Avenue, New York, NY 10010, USA
www.manchesteruniversitypress.co.uk

Distributed exclusively in the USA by
Palgrave, 175 Fifth Avenue, New York, NY 10010, USA

Distributed exclusively in Canada by
UBC Press, University of British Columbia, 2029 West Mall,
Vancouver, BC, Canada V6T 1Z2

British Library Cataloguing-in-Publication Data
A catalogue record for this book is available from the British Library

Library of Congress Cataloging-in-Publication Data applied for

ISBN 0 7190 6402 3 *hardback*
EAN 978 0 7190 6402 9
ISBN 0 7190 6403 1 *paperback*
EAN 978 0 7190 6403 6

First published 2006
15 14 13 12 11 10 09 08 07 06   10 9 8 7 6 5 4 3 2 1

Typeset in Aldus
by Koinonia, Manchester
Printed in Great Britain
by Bell & Bain Ltd, Glasgow

Contents

Acknowledgements

Towards the end of *The Woman Warrior*, Maxine Hong Kingston remarks that 'the beginning is hers, the ending mine'. It is with this conception of creative continuity in mind that I wish to thank Maxine Hong Kingston for her generosity in answering my questions during the writing of this book, and her graciousness when we met in London in October, 2003. I also wish to thank Professor Deborah Madsen and Professor A. Robert Lee for their generous help in defining this project in its early stages. The Bancroft Library, at the University of California, Berkeley, hosted me during April, 2005, when I consulted the Maxine Hong Kingston Papers, for which I am grateful. I would like to acknowledge the University of Wales, Aberystwyth, who awarded me a sabbatical in early 2005 to write this book. The Arts and Humanities Research Council gave me an award in 2005 which enabled completion of the project, which I acknowledge with gratitude. The University of Wales, Aberystwyth, University Research Fund awarded me a grant to visit Berkeley during Easter of 2005, and I acknowledge this assistance with gratitude. Professor John Thieme, Editor of the Contemporary World Writers Series, has been generous with his guidance and comments during various stages of writing this book, and I am very grateful to him. Matthew Frost gave me the opportunity to work with MUP again, and I would like to thank him. Dr Will Slocombe helped me to compile the Select Bibliography in this book, and I acknowledge his impeccable work with thanks.

On a personal note, I would like to mention my wonderful friends Kim, Elizabeth, Janet, Sera, Llinos and Jenny, who have all patiently let me rehearse my ideas, and bore each of them with my progress, over the last two years. I must also thank my husband Tim, for his endless patience, his astute and sensitively delivered commentary on my writing, lots of emergency childcare, too much chardonnay and many computer rescue missions over the last couple of years, and more. I owe you! Also, my dear daughter Mary, for her irreverent questions and for exhorting me to finish my homework early. Finally, this book is dedicated to my wonderful youngest daughter Madeleine, whose birth in February, 2003, was a joyful interruption to its progress.

Helena Grice
Aberystwyth

Series editor's foreword

Contemporary World Writers is an innovative series of authoritative introductions to a range of culturally diverse contemporary writers from outside Britain and the United States or from 'minority' backgrounds within Britain or the United States. In addition to providing comprehensive general introductions, books in the series also argue stimulating original theses, often but not always related to contemporary debates in post-colonial studies.

The series locates individual writers within their specific cultural contexts, while recognising that such contexts are themselves invariably a complex mixture of hybridised influences. It aims to counter tendencies to appropriate the writers discussed into the canon of English or American literature or to regard them as 'other'.

Each volume includes a chronology of the writer's life, an introductory section on formative contexts and intertexts, discussion of all the writer's major works, a bibliography of primary and secondary works and an index. Issues of racial, national and cultural identity are explored, as are gender and sexuality. Books in the series also examine writers' use of genre, particularly ways in which Western genres are adapted or subverted and 'traditional' local forms are reworked in a contemporary context.

Contemporary World Writers aims to bring together the theoretical impulse which currently dominates post-colonial studies and closely argued readings of particular authors' works, and by so doing to avoid the danger of appropriating the specifics of particular texts into the hegemony of totalising theories.

Chronology

1940   Maxine Hong born to Chinese immigrants Tom and Ying Lan Hong in Stockton, California, on 27th October, the eldest of six children born to the couple in the United States. Two children born earlier died in China.

1955   Wins five-dollar prize from *Girl Scout Magazine* for essay, 'I Am an American'.

1958   Wins full scholarships to attend the University of California at Berkeley. Begins as an engineering major but changes to English. Graduates in 1962 with a B.A. in English.

1962   Marries actor Earll Kingston. Teaches high school English and maths.

1963   Gives birth to a son, Joseph Lawrence Chung Mei Kingston.

1967   With her husband and son leaves Berkeley to move to Hawai'i. Teaches high school and writes.

1976   Publishes *The Woman Warrior: Memoir of a Girlhood among Ghosts,* which wins the year's National Book Critics Circle Award for Nonfiction.

1977   Wins *Mademoiselle* Magazine Award. Wins National Education Association Award.

1978   Writes diaristic accounts that will later be published (in 1987) as *Hawai'i One Summer* in 'Hers' column. Wins Anisfield-Wolf Race Relations Award.

1979   *The Woman Warrior* is named by *Time* magazine as one of the top 10 nonfiction books of the decade.

1980   Publishes *China Men*. Named a 'Living Treasure of Hawai'i' by a Honolulu Buddhist sect. Endowment for the Arts writing fellow. *China Men* named to American Library Association Notable Books List.

1981   Wins National Book Award for Nonfiction for *China Men*. Nominated for a National Book Critics Circle Award, and is a finalist for the Pulitzer Prize for Nonfiction. The Bancroft Library, University of California, Berkeley, begins to compile a special collection of her papers.

1984   Visits China for the first time along with other writers, including Allen Ginsberg, Leslie Marmon Silko, Toni Morrison and Gary Snyder, sponsored by the University of California, Los Angeles, and as a guest of the Chinese Writers Association. Moves to Los Angeles.

1987   Publishes *Hawai'i One Summer* and *Through the Black Curtain*. Moves to Oakland, California.

1989   Publishes her first novel, *Tripmaster Monkey: His Fake Book*. PEN USA West award for fiction.

1990   Kingston is appointed a Chancellor's Distinguished Professor in the English Department at the University of California, Berkeley.

1991   *The Book of Peace*, a novel set during the Vietnam War, is destroyed in a fire that burns Kingston's Oakland Hills home to the ground. Kingston begins work on another book, which she tentatively titles *Another Book of Peace* or *The Fifth Book of Peace*. Kingston delivers the Martha Heasley Cox Lecture at San Jose State University.

1992   Kingston is inducted into the American Academy of Arts and Sciences.

1993   Receives Lila Wallace Reader's Digest Award, which Kingston uses to begin writing workshop for Vietnam veterans.

1995   Dramatised version of *The Woman Warrior* is named best play of the year by *USA Today*.

1997   Receives National Humanities Medal from President Bill Clinton.

1998   Receives Fred Cody Lifetime Achievement Award. Wins John Dos Passos Prize for Literature for *Tripmaster Monkey*.

1998   *Hawai'i One Summer* re-issued in paperback.

2000   Delivers the William E. Massey Sr. Lectures in the History of American Civilization at Harvard University.

2002   Publishes *To Be the Poet* based upon the William E. Massey Sr. Lectures in the History of American Civilization, delivered at Harvard University in 2000.

2003   Publishes *The Fifth Book of Peace*, her reconstructed lost novel.

Contexts and intertexts

I want to change the world through artistic pacifist means.
(Maxine Hong Kingston, 1991)

'The beginning is hers': the political and literary legacies of Maxine Hong Kingston

In 1989, Maxine Hong Kingston expressed her pleasure at the blossoming of Asian American literature: 'Something wonderful is happening right at this moment ... Amy Tan published *The Joy Luck Club*, and Hisaye Yamamoto published *Seventeen Syllables*, Frank Chin has a collection of short stories, and I think maybe Ruth-Anne Lumm McKunn just came out with her book on Chinese families. Jessica Hagedorn's in the spring, and Bharati Mukherjee is in the fall. She won the National Book Circle Critics Award. Something great must be going on'.[1] In 1990 she acknowledged that 'I do think I probably helped to inspire [this]'.[2] Some fourteen years later, her long awaited fifth book, appropriately entitled *The Fifth Book of Peace*, already promises to spawn as much critical debate, even controversy, as her earlier work. Since the publication of *The Woman Warrior* in 1976, Maxine Hong Kingston has gained a reputation as one of the most popular – and controversial – writers in the Asian American literary tradition, who has been by turn celebrated and excoriated. Kingston's development as a writer and cultural activist in relation to both ethnic and feminist traditions, occurs across the range of her expanding oeuvre: her two novels, her occasional writings and her two-book life-writing project. How do we account for the phenomenal success of *The Woman Warrior* – the most widely read title in American universities today – a success that not only propelled Kingston into the mainstream literary limelight, but also precipitated a vicious and ongoing controversy in Asian American letters over the authenticity, or fakery, of Kingston's cultural references? Why is it that Kingston's critics have so often solely concentrated on this dimension of her work? In this study, I will suggest that the debates over the veracity, or otherwise, of Kingston's cultural sources, and the vast body of critical material on the feminism–mother/daughter nexus in *The Woman Warrior*, has simultaneously obscured other, perhaps more pertinent and abiding preoccupations in Kingston's work. This book, then, will locate Kingston within two interconnected, specific cultural contexts: Chinese American history and politics; and the emergence of ethnic feminism in a post-civil rights era. It will contend that Kingston's body of work not only raises important questions concerning cultural authenticity, the role of different interpretive communities and canon formation, but that increasingly her oeuvre offers her readers a manifesto of pacifism for a contemporary era.

Maxine Hong Kingston and Amy Tan

The abiding critical focus on *The Woman Warrior* at the expense of the rest of Kingston's work I mention above has also ultimately been suggestive of a closer literary relationship between Kingston and her literary successor, the Chinese American woman writer Amy Tan, than can actually be identified. The twinning of Kingston and Tan as the literary purveyors of Chinese American mother-and-daughterhood has long since been ossified in delineations of the development of Asian American women's writing. The success of each writer on the basis of their contributions to and participations in American matrilineal discourse, though, is all the more remarkable when we consider that there is a gap of some thirteen years between the publication of their key narratives *The Woman Warrior*

(1976) and *The Joy Luck Club* (1989) respectively. Yet, in 1989, when *The Joy Luck Club* was published, *The Woman Warrior* was still on the trade paperback bestseller list. Obviously, there are similarities between Kingston and Tan beyond their success as Chinese American women writers. For instance, both writers have suffered from the contradictory reception of their first books: both were largely lauded for their work by mainstream reviewers and critics but at the same time received far more cautious reactions – and in Kingston's case some famously hostile ones (as I will later detail) – from Asian American writers and critics. In her seminal 1990 study, *Between Worlds: Women Writers of Chinese Ancestry*, Amy Ling reads the first novels of the pair together, and describes *The Joy Luck Club* as 'in parts an echo and a response and in parts a continuation and expansion' of *The Woman Warrior*.[3] The persistent focus upon mothers and daughters in both texts is clearly a similarity too tempting for many critics, who, like Wendy Ho, have noticed that 'Tan's book can fruitfully be compared to *The Woman Warrior*. As heroic paper daughters in quest of their mother's stories, Tan and Kingston empower not only their mothers but also themselves and their racial/ethnic communities through a psychic and oral/literary birthing that keeps alive the intimate, ever-changing record of tragedies, resistances, and joy luck for all people'.[4] Sau-ling Wong and Jeffery Santa-Ana write:

> It is not unusual to find readers who consider the two books practically synonymous with Asian American women's literature (or even Asian American literature), unbeholden to any context. It is much more productive, not to mention intellectually defensible, however, to understand them within the framework of Asian American women's writing, and their focus on mother–daughter relationships as part of a feminist agenda to preserve memory and establish a matrilineal tradition.[5]

Yet here are two writers who are less between worlds than of two separate ones. In terms of age, they are a generation apart: at 60-something, Maxine Hong Kingston could almost have literally as well as figuratively mothered the just-50 Amy Tan;

whereas Kingston grew up in the post-war environment of Stockton, California, Tan was just a child in the sixties. Kingston's academic life at Berkeley spanned the early to mid 1960s, and so her involvement and interest in ethnic, pacifist and feminist activism occurred at the same time as a period of especially vigorous political activity on the University of California, Berkeley campus. Each writer has also followed a different physical trajectory. Kingston is a California writer, and she has even been anthologised in collections of writing about California and the West Coast (despite heading for Hawai'i at the height of Vietnam). Tan was born in Oakland, California, and grew up there, despite a sojourn in Switzerland with her family. Of the two, Tan is considerably better known in a commercial sense, and her novels have had more popular appeal than Kingston's. Kingston has undoubtedly had more critical acclaim, and is more likely to appear on university and college curricula. It is now lore in Asian American circles that Kingston is the most widely taught living writer in US colleges today.

All that said, the phenomenal success of Amy Tan's book *The Joy Luck Club* – and probably her later novels published in the 1990s and 2000s – must nevertheless partly be attributed to *The Woman Warrior*'s concern with feminist issues such as emerging womanhood, identity and self, which helped to create a market for mother–daughter writing. The coupling of *The Woman Warrior* and *The Joy Luck Club* in critical discourse also rests upon the perceived similarity of narrative perspective upon issues of inter-cultural (mis)understanding. This obscures a real difference in narrative approach and complexity though; what has been characterised elsewhere as *The Woman Warrior*'s sophisticated 'interrogative modality' versus *The Joy Luck Club*'s 'declarative', epistemologically less problematic, narrative mode. In fact, it is the formal complexity of *The Woman Warrior*, and the challenges it poses as a studied text, which largely account for its ubiquity in critical explorations of auto/biography, feminist self-inscription, women's self-actualisation and maternality.[6]

The bind of the mother–daughter nexus, or, where it all began

The appearance of *The Woman Warrior* on the literary landscape in 1976 caused nothing less than a revolution in Asian American literary and feminist studies. It became an almost immediate crossover hit, winning several awards in its year of publication, and virtually guaranteeing Kingston a celebrated place as the undisputed sovereign of Asian American writing.[7] But its impact did not end there. Since 1976, *The Woman Warrior* 'has generated a veritable industry of critical analysis';[8] and has subsequently spawned a whole new sub-genre of Asian American fiction: the fiction of matrilineage.

The evolution of a tradition of writing about matrilineage within Asian American studies also coincided with a growth of interest in the mother–daughter dyad by mainstream feminist writers. It is important to note that the year which saw the publication of Kingston's text was the same year that a series of seminal feminist publications appeared: Adrienne Rich's *Of Woman Born: Motherhood as Institution and as Experience*, Dorothy Dinnerstein's *The Mermaid and the Minotaur*, and Jean Baker Miller's *Toward a New Psychology of Women*. Years immediately preceding these witnessed Betty Friedan's *The Feminist Mystique* (1963), Kate Millet's *Sexual Politics*, Shulamith Firestone's *The Dialectic of Sex* and Anne Koedt's *The Myth of the Vaginal Orgasm* (all 1970). Within the realm of literature, feminist fiction such as Marge Piercy's *Woman on the Edge of Time* was also published in 1976. So, *The Woman Warrior* emerged co-terminously with the emergence of feminist fiction, and at the height of feminist theorising, in America. But was this just coincidence?[9]

Although the development of Asian American feminism shares a genealogy with mainstream feminism, at the same time it both lags behind and departs from it. Contemporaneous with the consolidation of feminist agendas both within and beyond academia, women of colour were engaged in a project to both dismantle patriarchal paradigms and to question white feminism's race blindness.[10] As Nellie Wong paradigmatically asked, 'How can we separate our race from our sex, our sex from our race?' Maxine Hong Kingston's writing occupies an especially important place in the recent history of feminist thought, in particular the watershed period of the late 1970s and early 1980s when many mainstream feminist thinkers were becoming aware (or at least were being made aware) of the insularity of some of their traditional frames of reference, acknowledging that issues of gender cannot be separated from those of ethnicity, class and culture. In many ways, Kingston's work is symptomatic of a feminist understanding of *all* identities as mobile and continually open to re-negotiation. For instance, the treatment of gender identity in Kingston's writing encompasses a whole series of boundary crossings: the contradictory and conflicting definitions of womanhood that a Chinese American woman is forced to confront and the complexities of gender identity for Chinese American women, given their exoticisation by WASP culture. As woman of colour feminist movements began to challenge mainstream feminism in this period, so ethnic feminist texts like Kingston's began to gain prominence and attention from white feminist readers too, and something of a two-way exchange began to occur.[11] Much of this early feminist work centred upon issues of maternity, as an integral part of female identity and as a metaphor of feminism itself. For example, the Asian American contributions to the major 1981 ethnic feminist anthology, *This Bridge Called My Back: Writings by Radical Women of Color*, often included a focus upon issues of motherhood, such as: Nellie Wong's essay on growing up; Genny Lim's piece on versions of womanhood; Mitsuye Yamada's pieces on the hardships of her mother's life and the connections between motherhood and stereotyping; and Merle Woo's 'Letter to Ma', in which she explicitly addressed the complexities of the mother–daughter relationship.

The impact of *The Woman Warrior* undoubtedly helped to create a new commercial market for Asian American books about maternality, and since 1976 many Asian American texts have been published which to a greater or lesser extent, focus upon mothering and daughtering. In addition to Amy Tan's novels, these include: Joy Kogawa's *Obasan* (1981); SKY Lee's *Disappearing Moon Café* (1990); Gail Tsukiyama's *Women of the Silk* (1991); Julie Shigekuni's *A Bridge Between Us* (1995) and Anita Rau Badami's *Tamarind Mem* (1996). Other texts have taken mother *loss* as their theme, such as Theresa Hak Kyung Cha's *Dictee* (1982); Adeline Yen Mah's *Falling Leaves: The Story of an Unwanted Chinese Daughter* (1997); Patti Kim's *A Cab Called Reliable* (1997) and Lois-Ann Yamanaka's *Blu's Hanging* (1997). Nevertheless, Kingston cannot be said to have single-handedly spawned a revival in Asian American women's writing; nor, as Sau-ling Wong reminds us, can the invention of Chinese American matrilineal discourse be solely attributed to *The Woman Warrior*. As Wong writes, although *The Joy Luck Club* is 'something of an accessible "*Woman Warrior* without tears"', Tan is 'not so much revisiting Kingston territory as sharing a concern long of interest to many other Chinese American women writers'.[12] Wong cites several antecedents to Kingston, including Helena Kuo's *I've Come a Long Way* (1942) and Jade Snow Wong's *Fifth Chinese Daughter* (1945). Elsewhere, in an article aptly entitled 'Chinese American Women Writers: The Tradition Behind Maxine Hong Kingston' (1990), Amy Ling also refers to works by Han Suyin, Lin Tai-yi, the Eaton sisters, Mai-mai Sze, the Lin sisters, Janet Lim, Virginia Lee, Diana Chang and Anna Chennault, and wryly comments that 'Kingston is not an isolated Athena'.[13]

If this seems an overly schematic way to approach the theoretical and creative impact of *The Woman Warrior* (or, perhaps more accurately, to dispute it), then this is due to the tendency both within Asian American feminist criticism and in feminist literary criticism of Kingston's work more generally, to characterise the evolution of Asian American matrilineal discourse as 'pre- and post-*Woman Warrior*', as Sau-ling Wong puts it.[14] Indeed, delineations of Asian American feminist writing almost always pinpoint the publication of Kingston's text as *the* pivotal moment in its maturation, from Shirley Lim's seminal essay, 'Asian American Daughters Rewriting Asian

Maternal Texts' (1991) onwards.[15] This is partly, of course, a political imperative; as Wong puts it: 'Identifying a matrilineal Asian American tradition is important in terms of not only racial politics within feminism, but also gender politics within cultural nationalism'.[16] It is for this reason, too, that Kingston's later, and arguably more experimental, book, *Tripmaster Monkey: His Fake Book* (1989), has been largely overlooked in Asian American critical discourse, since it was not just overshadowed by Kingston's life-writing volumes, but was also eclipsed by Tan's *The Joy Luck Club*, which appeared in the same year.

In her study, *In Her Mother's House: The Politics of Asian American Mother–Daughter Writing*, Wendy Ho is in no doubt about the importance of Kingston's matrilineal writing. In a discussion which also includes Amy Tan and Fae Myenne Ng, author of *Bone* (1993), Ho writes:

> In representing the painful struggle of mothers and daughters to articulate the social spaces for themselves and for their interactions, Kingston, Tan, and Ng portray a vibrant, contentious, and vital women's subjectivity-, culture-, and history-in-the-making.[17]

Ho suggests that one result of Kingston's success is that an Asian American female readership has dramatically increased, and that publishing houses have been quick to respond through the targeted marketing of new writers. In many of the advance reviews of Ng's 1993 novel, *Bone*, and Chinese Canadian novelist SKY Lee's *Disappearing Moon Café* (1990), for instance, comparisons were drawn with both Kingston's and Amy Tan's work.

If the thematic content of *The Woman Warrior* has spawned a myriad of imitations, then it is equally true that what became known simply as 'the book' has bequeathed a formal legacy as well.[18] It is well documented that the novelty of the interconnected 'talk-story' structure of *The Woman Warrior* troubled its critics but caught the imagination of its readers. In her book, *Transcultural Reinventions: Asian American and Asian Canadian Short-story Cycles*, Rocío G. Davis speaks of this as an 'experiment of intergenre synthesis', and we may well attribute some of the distinctiveness and impact of the text to this experimentation.[19] As Davis points out, many ethnic texts in particular, mirror, even imitate, Kingston's formal experimentation: African American Gloria Naylor's *The Women of Brewster Place* (1980); Chicana Sandra Cisneros's *The House on Mango Street* (1984), and Native American Louise Erdrich's *Love Medicine* (1993), to name but three, as well as other Asian American examples: Sylvia Watanabe's *Talking to the Dead* (1992); Lois-Ann Yamanaka's *Wild Meat and the Bully Burgers* (1996), and Rachna Mara's *Of Customs and Excise* (1991), for instance.

A further legacy concerns the interface between text and society. Most of Kingston's writings have been primarily read as personal stories – of coming-of-age or maturation, of familial relationships or ancestral connectivity. But these are also stories of both community and culture. Bonnie TuSmith has described how the creation and perpetuation of ethnically specific mythologies and cultural artefacts plays a key role in the establishment and consolidation of ethnic communities.[20] Kingston's complex re-workings of Chinese/American mythologised versions of femininity and womanhood, and her re-inscription of female roles of mothering and daughtering in *The Woman Warrior* as well as the 'fathering' that we see in *China Men*, have undoubtedly promulgated a range of Asian American role models and literary character-types, and especially female ones.[21] In her study *Betrayal and other Acts of Subversion* (2001), Leslie Bow identifies: the woman-as-transgressor, the woman who's-witnessed-women's-oppression-at-close-quarter, the woman-who's-transcended-a-bad-marriage, the woman-who-endures and even 'ethnic grandma', to name but five.[22] Bow explains this replication slightly differently:

> An identifiable plot structure … appears in women's texts across Asian American ethnicities … in this feminist narrative, a previous generation of women's experiences serve as a foundation, albeit a traumatic one, authorizing a better future. The effect of coming to this consciousness is both

didactic (e.g., I learn from my mother's oppression) and salutary (e.g., I can be healed by challenging the restrictions she once faced), producing the idea of a transnational, transhistorical women's community that exposes patriarchy.[23]

The woman-who-endures is a particularly pervasive character type, what Bow calls 'a moment of popularizing narratives of women's trauma',[24] from Akemi Kikumura's *Through Harsh Winters: The Life of a Japanese* (1981) and Helie Lee's *Still Life with Rice* (1996) to Patricia Chao's *Monkey King* (1997) and Nora Okja Keller's *Comfort Woman* (1997). Another type identified by Monica Chiu in her study *Filthy Fictions* (2004) is the character representing 'women's promiscuity amid an authoritarian adherence with tradition' in books such as Ginu Kamani's *Junglee Girl* (1995), a type which is clearly traceable to Kingston's No Name Woman.[25] Just as *The Woman Warrior*'s No Name Woman bloodies the ancestral homestead and forever stains the family's history, so, as Chiu explores, many women characters in contemporary Asian American fiction, by way of their bodies, leak, dirty and muddy their environments and communities.[26]

Kingston's postfeminism

Despite the foregoing, it is not enough to simply designate Kingston as a product of sixties counterculture and second-wave feminism, though, and to suggest that writers like Amy Tan and Fae Myenne Ng have simply followed in her wake. The nature of feminism and other cultural movements has changed immeasurably since 1976. One development is the emergence of postfeminism. Roughly dated as corresponding to the latter 1980s and the 1990s, postfeminism is defined by Ann Brooks as 'the theoretical meeting ground between feminism and antifoundationalist movements such as postcolonialism', and, as such, it seeks to 'challenge [the] hegemonic assumptions held by second wave feminist epistemologies'.[27] A watershed period of development, then, which saw a critical engagement on the part of the mainstream and women-of-colour movements with 'earlier feminist political and theoretical concepts and strategies as a result of its engagements with other social movements for change'.[28] In other words, the ten years between 1980 and 1990 – which broadly corresponds to the time lag between the publication of The Woman Warrior and The Joy Luck Club – saw significant alterations in the landscape of feminism, and notably its increased imbrication with other social movements for change. On the surface, it might be assumed that whereas Kingston's feminism stemmed from the second wave, Amy Tan's, or Fae Myenne Ng's, writing would bear the hallmark of postfeminism, but in actuality this is not the case. Maxine Hong Kingston's long-standing coterminous interest in women's issues, pacifism, civil rights and theories of social responsibility, in fact prematurely ushered her brand of feminism into the realm of postfeminism, which was only to emerge as a wide-spread phenomenon much later. It is worth noting, for instance, that Kingston was identified as a key figure in Chela Sandoval's 1991 retrospective essay on 'U.S. Third World Feminism', which was identified as a post-1971 phenomenon, and which also included Toni Morrison, Leslie Marmon Silko, Barbara Smith, Rosara Sanchez and Theresa Hak Kyung Cha.[29] In contrast, Amy Tan, Fae Myenne Ng and other Asian American women writing in the mother/daughter tradition have never really been recognised as conspicuously feminist writers; instead they are usually rather sloppily identified with a hazily defined 1990s feminism by dint of the overlap of thematic concerns in their writing with women's issues such as inter-generational female relationships, marriage, mothering and both sexual and financial autonomy, the sum of which cannot really be said to amount to any kind of feminist advocacy.

After China: Kingston's China imaginings

As much as she is a writer in the 'post' of feminism, Maxine Hong Kingston is also a writer 'after China'. She was born and raised in the United States and only visited China as an adult.

She is also, then, a writer of diaspora; a second-generation Chinese American, born soon after the arrival in the United States of her parents. China was always already nothing more or less than a fiction: a familially mediated imaginary entity which seemed to represent an unseen, unknown code of acceptable and prohibited behaviour and mysterious cultural ritual and an, at times, alien language. Much of her fictional output has been concerned with the vagaries of Chinese culture from the American child-narrator's perspective, and she has made much literary capital out of the stuff of diaspora. Think of Kingston's elegant descriptions of journeys to the Gold Mountain undertaken by her Chinese male forbears, or the many linguistic puns and jokes of *The Woman Warrior*. But to be 'after China' is also to revisit it, and for this American, Californian, West Coast writer, China – in its political, historical and cultural manifestations – remains an on-going preoccupation as both source and subject.

Kingston refers to China as 'a country I made up'.[30] Her constant and principal focus in her life-writing has been the history of Chinese *American* immigration, but in her exploration of this subject she assumes a degree of knowledge on the part of her readers about China and its history of engagement with the US, since China's recent history is one of the determinants of her own parents' immigration to America in the 1930s. As she has said of her relationship with China: 'I feel directly concerned'.[31] The early years of Kingston's life coincided with the last years of the Nationalist–Communist conflict in China and the establishment of the People's Republic of China in 1949. The period of Communist consolidation and reform in the 1950s and early 1960s had a far-reaching, even devastating effect on much of China (Kingston's family included), and this is something to which she refers repeatedly in both *The Woman Warrior* and *China Men*. It is clear that the Cultural Revolution also devastated her family:

> The news from China has been confusing ... I was nine years old when the letters made my parents, who are rocks, cry. My father screamed in his sleep. My mother wept and crumpled up the letters. She set fire to them page

by page in the ashtray, but new letters came almost everyday. The only letters they opened without fear were the ones with red borders, the holiday letters that mustn't carry bad news. The other letters said that my uncles were made to kneel on broken glass during their trials and had confessed to being landowners. They were all executed.[32]

Kingston's interest in China at this time stretches to an examination of the history of Chinese–American interaction, both in encounters on the international stage and the ways in which this dictated the fortunes of Chinese immigrants to America. Of her books, *China Men* is most thoroughly concerned with this history, even famously switching narrative mode half-way through to include a chronology of the legislation which has adversely affected Chinese Americans. Both *The Woman Warrior* and *China Men* also bear the distinct hallmark of a cold war America in the 1950s, which lasted until Richard Nixon's visit to China in 1972.[33] Of her family's relationship to China, Kingston has remarked:

> The older generation feel it's a very terrible place. If any of us go, something bad will happen to us. We will get killed or something. In my family, just about all the men were killed in the revolution. The other fear is that we'll be thought of as Communist sympathizers if we go and if there is a McCarthy type witchhunt, we will be thrown in relocation camps. There is a whole weight of history involved here.[34]

Kingston does not see a clear distinction between the historical events in China and her family's fortunes in America though; rather she instead figures the two as inevitably interlinked, conceived more as a global phenomenon, as she tells her mother, 'We belong to the planet now'.[35]

Kingston's peace project

Kingston's commitment to a global conception of humanity is intertwined with her abiding promotion of pacifism, a preoccupation that has become increasingly manifest in her work, and which culminated in *The Fifth Book of Peace*, which appeared in 2003. Of this project, she said: 'What I wanted to do was ... write a global novel'.[36] One could be forgiven for thinking that Kingston's interest lies in war, since her writing makes such frequent references to wars that have occurred in different points in history. A brief tally finds references to the Chinese–British Opium War, the Chinese–Japanese War of 1894–95, the Korean War, World War II and of course the Vietnam War. In reality, this simply reflects her desire to explore all possible avenues of peaceful activism in relation to a whole range of political themes, of which war, racism, gender inequality and violence are only the most obvious. As she observes, 'I think it's pretty terrible, but in everybody's living experience, there's been a war, whether you've actually fought in it in another country, or whether you were here suffering or participating in another way'.[37] This brings us to Kingston's possibly greatest legacy as a writer, which is her consistently politicised worldview and commitment to pacifism in all its forms, which constitutes a personal and writerly credo; as she notes: 'it takes a whole life to organize and demonstrate'.[38] Each of her books has taken pacifism as its theme, to a greater or lesser degree. *The Woman Warrior* explores China's involvement in a series of wars, as they impacted upon her family in China and in America; *Hawai'i One Summer* includes an essay entitled 'War'; *China Men* and *The Fifth Book of Peace* both meditate extensively upon the personal and political fallout of Vietnam; and *Tripmaster Monkey* focuses upon the options available to a draft-age activist in Berkeley in the sixties, against the backdrop of the devastating events unfolding in Vietnam. In an interview with Diane Simmons, Kingston expressed her belief that stories are the conduit for passing on social responsibility;[39] and of her own sense of her role as a writer, she asserts:

> I'm beginning to see that it may be the obligation of artists to have a vision of a future. We need an idea before we can create who we are and what our society is. It seems to me there's a horrible emergency right now. We seem to be on

the brink of destroying everything. And it seems I have this power to envision a healthy society, healthy human beings, and I need to maybe create new myths.[40]

Legacy or heritage?

In a passage late in *The Woman Warrior*, Kingston describes the ancient Chinese forbidden stitch, that knot so complex it blinds the embroiderer, and thus was outlawed. Kingston tells us that 'If I had lived in China, I would have been an outlaw knot-maker'.[41] This oft-quoted analogy of the forbidden stitch has become a metaphor for the once hidden/forbidden creativity of Asian American women. In the 1989 anthology of the same name, editor Shirley Geok-lin Lim cites Kingston's rendition of the knotmaker's story and announces a new era for the Asian American female artisan, one in which 'younger Asian American women writers have inherited the scene' set by Kingston in 1976.[42] Lim's use of the word 'inheritance' to characterise the influence of Kingston is not insignificant. Here, this inheritance is summed up by Asian American activist and writer, Phoebe Eng:

> *The Woman Warrior* gave young Asian American women a voice. It legitimized our issues. We learned in *The Woman Warrior* that each of us has the ability to fight when aggression is needed, and to create when life is good. But *The Woman Warrior* offered only a starting point. We learned how to be young girls then, but now, we need to talk about adulthood, with all of its issues and choices.[43]

In evaluating Maxine Hong Kingston, perhaps, rather than thinking in terms of legacy, we would be better to speak of heritage. Legacy implies a gift left behind, whereas heritage carries with it connotations of something precious passed down through generations, something continuing into the future.

The Woman Warrior (1976)

Politically and socially … I look at myself as being very much a feminist. Growing up as I did as a kid, I don't see how I could not have been a feminist. In Chinese culture, people always talk about how girls are bad. When you hear that, right away it makes you radical like anything. (Maxine Hong Kingston)[1]

Maureen Sabine's innovative 2004 study of *The Woman Warrior* and *China Men, Maxine Hong Kingston's Broken Book of Life: An Intertextual Study*, explores the disproportionate strength of the feminist perspective in *The Woman Warrior* and suggests that this has obscured Kingston's other political and thematic concerns. Sabine argues that both books should be read together as a diptych, since as a whole they constitute a conversation between her male and female forbears, a 'broken book' of and about life: hers, her relatives' and, expanding out, the contemporary life of Chinese Americans in the United States.[2] Sabine's concept of the 'broken book' is an apposite way to approach a book so overburdened by critical commentary that as Sau-ling Wong observes, it

is a daunting task. As one of the most widely circulated and frequently taught literary texts by a living American author, *The Woman Warrior* has generated a vast scholarship. This critical output, furthermore, represents a range of often antagonistic views on the book's meaning and significance: as with its counterparts in other American 'ethnic canons,' *The Woman Warrior* has been steeped in controversy, enthusiastically claimed, ingeniously deployed, and at times bitterly denounced by contesting interpretive communities. Anyone attempting to profile its complex reception history must therefore be prepared to give a reasonably intelligible account of how she got from hundreds of titles to a handful of article-length studies.[3]

Nearly thirty years have now passed since the publication of Kingston's first, and still most successful, book. As Wong notes, published to wide critical acclaim, it has since spawned countless articles and books, as well as arousing intense debates about such issues as genre and feminist writing. At the time of writing this book, the MLA online database listed 376 articles solely on *The Woman Warrior*; Amazon.com lists 148 critical studies on *The Woman Warrior*; while many other books and articles contain sections on the book to a lesser or greater degree. Anthony J. Fonseca observes that Kingston is 'the most influential Asian American writer of the twentieth century' and *The Woman Warrior* is 'the yardstick against which Asian American writers are measured'.[4] In *Compositional Subjects: Enfiguring Asian/ American Women* Laura Hyun Yi Kang goes even further, describing *The Woman Warrior* as one of a select few 'disciplinary brand names' in academia, locating Kingston along with the likes of Chaucer, Milton and Shakespeare.[5] Much of the critical debate surrounding *Warrior* has centred upon the book's troubling generic status. Ostensibly a memoir – the subtitle is 'Memoirs of a Girlhood among Ghosts' – the book won the National Book Critics Circle Award for nonfiction, but it blends together elements of several genres, including fiction, myth, auto/biography and memoir, in a manner that is not easily categorised.

The Woman Warrior's critical controversy

I may want to write tragedy, not a guide-to-Chinatown.
(Maxine Hong Kingston, Letter to Shawn Wong, December,
1976)

In the years immediately following *Warrior*'s publication,
Kingston was extensively attacked for what several critics saw as
her misuse of generic categories. The Chinese American critic
and playwright Frank Chin, for example, accused Kingston of
reinforcing white fantasies about Chinese Americans;[6] reviewer
Benjamin Tong charged Kingston with writing a 'fashionable
feminist work written with white acceptance in mind';[7] and the
Chinese American writer Jeffery Chan berated Kingston's pub-
lisher, Knopf, for categorising *The Woman Warrior* as biography when, he argued, it was self-evidently fictional.[8] A more
sensitively nuanced criticism came from Chinese American
Katheryn M. Fong, in an open letter to Kingston:

> I am bothered by your distortions of the histories of China
> and Chinese America. Your story is a *very personal* des-
> cription of growing up in Chinese America. ... I read your
> references to mythical and feudal China as fiction – as
> descriptions of ghost-dream imaginings of a child who
> heard stories of an unknown place called China. Your
> fantasy stories are embellished versions of your mother's
> embellished versions of stories. As fiction, these stories
> are creatively written with graphic imagery and emotion.
> The problem is that non-Chinese are reading your fiction
> as true accounts of Chinese and Chinese American
> history. That's the awesome price we Chinese Americans
> pay when so few of us – Jade Snow Wong, yourself, and a
> few others – are published. Your one experience, your one
> story, becomes the definitive description of all of us.
> Chinese Americans have commonalities, but I hardly
> think we are so homogeneous.[9]

Kingston herself has largely stayed out of these debates, which
have become known as the 'Chinese American pen wars',
although she is well aware that she has become a representative

voice, especially for an Asian American female community, as she remarked to Karen Amano:

> I saw myself as finding and creating my own individual voice, but at the same time it is also the voice of Asian-American people. It's also the voice of all those people such as the No Name Aunt. This is a person with no voice. She died a long time ago without a voice, and I, through my own voice, can give her one. I can give voice to people who have no political voice, who have no personal voice; it's possible to give them a voice through my own work. So it is both individual and it's a universal or racial voice.[10]

In a 1976 letter to fellow writer Shawn Wong, she expanded upon her own mission and her reaction to her critics:

> I have been noticing what the critics label it and where the book stores shelve it – and the lack of pigeon-holing is delightful: I've seen it under fiction, non-fiction, sociology, anthropology, biography, woman's lit, Chinese, Asian, general. This confusion really makes me feel good. I am glad that the word 'memoirs' does *not*, as Frank says, automatically mean 'autobiography'.[11]

In a later letter in the same correspondence, she had the final word:

> But why should all these critics have to think about whether or not the book is 'typical'? Why do I have to 'represent' anyone? … None of these writers point out how and why this book is different, but merely point out its difference as a flaw.[12]

The much-debated generic identity of *The Woman Warrior* and the 'pen wars' surrounding its reception also raise the question – or more accurately the problem – of readership for many ethnic writers. Much of the criticism levelled at *The Woman Warrior* by Asian American critics like Frank Chin, Ben Tong and Jeffery Chan, ensued from their belief in the responsibilities, as they saw them, of the ethnic writer to his or her ethnic community. This view had been set out prior to the publication of *The Woman Warrior*, in a manifesto for Asian American writers, authored by Frank Chin together with Jeffery Paul Chan, Lawson Fusao Inada and Shawn H. Wong, in the introduction to their anthology of Asian American writing, *Aiiieeee!* (1974). In this piece, these authors' ideas about cultural and generic purity versus the 'contamination' to be found in texts like Kingston's, were linked to the idea of the 'ideal' Asian American writer as *über*-masculine: he (and it is mainly a 'he') ought to combat racist stereotyping of Asian Americans as emasculated Charlie Chan figures. (This combative view of writing obviously has ironic resonances in Kingston's own work on the figure of the woman warrior.) These and other critics who have condemned Kingston for her failure to render Chinese language, myths and traditions accurately, suggest that she has 'failed' to represent faithfully the socio-historical reality of the experience of Chinese Americans (as they see it) in her work. All these charges rest upon an understanding of the ethnic writer's role in her community as an ambassador to white society, with a duty to her 'own' ethnic group. They also proceed from a hyper-awareness of the gaze of an Anglo society readership. Kingston's whole-hearted rejection of such responsibilities attests to her self-styled role as an ethnic 'trickster', manipulating literary tools like the myths she rewrites as a means of avoiding precisely the kind of ethnic pigeonholing about which the *Aiiieeee!* critics and others have been so anxious. *The Woman Warrior* masquerades as a series of different kinds of writing, without ever faithfully fulfilling the readerly expectations of any one mode. In so doing, it addresses different readerships by turns. Kingston has discussed how her use of cultural reference points like the Fa Mu Lan myth (discussed below) allows her to interpolate, or exclude, certain groups of readers at different stages in her narrative. Genre acts as one such reference point in the text, which suggests itself as autobiography, myth or fiction in turn.

Adolescent girlhood and the coming-of-age narrative

> As long as women are still not equal with men, then we need Fa Mu Lan as our mythic heroine. (Maxine Hong Kingston, interview with Karen Amano)

> Whenever she had to warn us about life, my mother told stories ... a story to grow up on. (*The Woman Warrior*)

The Woman Warrior recounts the childhood experiences of a young girl who is caught between her ancestral Chinese/ Cantonese culture and the American culture of her upbringing in Stockton, California. Kingston juxtaposes and interweaves her adolescent perspective with a retrospective adult commentary upon her experiences. The text is split into five stories, each episode tracking Kingston's theme of the development of the young girl into the inspirational figure of the woman warrior. Each section relates the story of a particular woman who is formative in the narrator's life, and these maternal figures are both actual and mythical, ghostly and real presences in the young girl's life.[13]

The narrative opens with an injunction to silence: 'You must not tell anyone', Kingston's mother warns her, before going on to recount the true story of Kingston's aunt's illegitimate pregnancy, shame and eventual suicide.[14] This 'no name aunt' hovers as an absent presence throughout Kingston's story, serving to reinforce the sense of an almost overwhelming burden of Chinese patriarchal culture on the women in the text. This initial section thus starts to explore the debilitating effects of Chinese patriarchal culture upon women, a theme that is threaded throughout the text. The 'no name aunt' became a victim of the Chinese village community that ostracised her after she became pregnant. Ultimately, she drowned herself and her newborn in the drinking-water well. Her story is told to the young narrator by her mother as a cautionary tale: it is both a warning not to humiliate her parents, by becoming pregnant herself, but also, and more crucially, it serves as an injunction against passing on this story of familial shame (*WW*, p. 13). The narrator, though, makes her own use of this tale: as a 'story to grow up on', she uses her aunt's biography as an inspirational emancipatory narrative, preferring to view her aunt as less of a failure and more as a heroine who successfully wrought vengeance upon those who spurned and controlled her, by throwing her body into the family drinking well, and thus contaminating the village's only water source (*WW*, p. 13). Rather than obeying her mother, the young Kingston tells her aunt's tale, although at the same time she recognises the perils attendant upon that telling, as she notes too that her aunt 'does not always mean me well' (*WW*, p. 22). This opening section demonstrates the young girl's ability to sift through the cultural fragments that she inherits via her mother and to make use of them for her own purposes. However, she recognises the confusions and contradictions that she faces in separating out her two worlds: 'Chinese-Americans', she asks, 'when you try to understand what things in you are Chinese, how do you separate what is peculiar to childhood, to poverty, insanities, one family, your mother who marked your growing with stories, from what is Chinese? What is Chinese tradition and what is the movies?' (*WW*, p. 13).

The second section, 'White Tigers', introduces the no name woman's counterpart in the text, the mythical and legendary character of Fa Mu Lan, or the woman warrior. The narrator's mother, Brave Orchid, also tells this story. Brave Orchid's ambivalence in guiding and instructing her daughter is that on one hand, she offers her daughter emancipatory narratives of female avengers, such as the woman warrior, but on the other, she stresses the perils and pitfalls of womanhood through the narrative of the no name woman. Kingston notes: 'When we Chinese girls listened to the adults talking-story, we learned that we failed if we grew up to be but wives or slaves. We could be heroines, swordswomen' (*WW*, p. 25). The young girl's dilemma is that she must decide whether to become a woman warrior, or a no-name woman, and thereby reconcile the two visions of her ancestral culture that she receives via these narratives. Highlighting this contradiction, the narrator says of her mother: 'She said I would grow up a wife and a slave, but she taught me the song of the warrior woman' (*WW*, p. 26).

The young girl resolutely chooses to become a woman warrior. Fa Mu Lan's escapades are given central significance in the narrative, and are related in a quasi-mythical manner, with Fa Mu Lan herself handling the story in the first person. This strategy accentuates the young girl's heightened identification with her heroine. The character of Fa Mu Lan is loosely based upon the Chinese 'Ballad of Mulan', as Sau-ling C. Wong has noted.[15] However, as Wong goes on to point out, Fa Mu Lan has 'gained the status of a topos' in Chinese literature, and there are many different versions of the story.[16] Kingston's own version should be read as a fantasy, as the whole 'White Tigers' section of the text is meant to function in a mythic and non-naturalistic way. As Kingston herself has noted: 'Fa Mu Lan is a fantasy that inspires the girls' psyches and their politics. The myths transform lives and are themselves changed.'[17] Although Kingston has moulded the myth to suit her purposes, the version of the Fa Mu Lan story that we find in *The Woman Warrior* is faithful to some of the basic plot elements of the story, whilst changing others. Traditional versions, as Sau-ling Wong explains it, tend to emphasise the character's battles and hardships as a woman warrior, rather than her transformation into a warrior-figure.[18] Kingston's story, unlike traditional versions, opens with the childhood heroine's encounter with an old couple who train her in martial arts, skills essential for her transformation into a woman warrior. Part of this training is the girl's endurance test in the land of the white tigers, which gives this section of the text its name. She must survive without food, shelter or warmth in an inhospitable climate alongside the white tigers as a rite of passage in her transformation into the figure of the woman warrior. She then leaves her mentors and teachers in the mountains and returns to her village, ready to avenge the wrongs done to her family and fellow villagers. Kingston has also added the next section of the tale, when Fa Mu Lan's parents carve a list of grievances onto her back, which it is her mission to avenge (this story is thus melded with another fable, that of the warrior

Ngak Fei). Thus equipped, Fa Mu Lan gathers an army of village men and, disguised as a man herself, leads her army to victory after victory, pausing only long enough to give birth to her child. Kingston's version ends, in line with traditional versions, with the woman warrior returning to live a life of filial piety with her parents-in-law.

Many of the elements of the Fa Mu Lan story added by Kingston correspond to fragments of other and equally well-known parables. Thus, the back-carving incident corresponds to the popular story of Ngak Fei, a male heroic figure who has characters carved on his back by his mother, also demanding his service in honour of his kinspeople. Similarly, many elements of Kingston's Fa Mu Lan story reflect classical Chinese narratives of warrior revenge and peasant revolution. These connections have led many commentators to lament Kingston's inability to render Chinese myths and parables faithfully in her work. As she herself has observed, many pirate translations and editions of the novel have 'corrected' the 'errors' to be found in her version of the Fa Mu Lan story. In responding to these complaints, Kingston retorted:

> Sinologists have criticised me for not knowing myths and for distorting them; pirates correct my myths, revising them to make them conform to some traditional Chinese version. They don't understand that myths have to change, be useful or be forgotten. Like the people who carry them across oceans, the myths become American. The myths I write are new, American. That's why they often appear as cartoons and kung fu movies. I take the power I need from whatever myth. Thus Fa Mu Lan has the words cut into her back; in traditional story, it is the man, Ngak Fei the Patriot, whose parents cut vows on his back. I mean to take his power for women.[19]

The Fa Mu Lan story is immediately juxtaposed by Kingston with this comment on the narrator's own life: 'My American life has been such a disappointment' (*WW*, p. 47). By connecting the young girl's life to that of Fa Mu Lan at this moment, Kingston shifts the narrative perspective from a mythical mode focusing upon the woman warrior to that of her mother, Brave Orchid. It is at this point in the text that we see the Chinese American daughter struggling to reconcile the paradoxical versions of femininity and identity with which she is confronted via her mother's stories and teachings. On the one hand, she is inured to hearing Chinese sayings such as 'Feeding girls is feeding cowbirds', whilst on the other hand, she listens to her mother 'talking-story' about Fa Mu Lan (*WW*, p. 48). On the one hand, she busies herself turning 'American-feminine, or no dates', whilst on the other, she 'went away to college – Berkeley in the sixties – and I studied, and I marched to save the world' (*WW*, p. 49). On the one hand, she tells us that there 'is a Chinese word for the female *I* – which is "slave". Break the women with their own tongues!' whilst on the other, she imagines her own revenge upon racism and sexism:

> To avenge my family, I'd have to storm across China to take back our farm from the Communists; I'd have to rage across the United States to take back the laundry in New York and the one in California. ... A descendant of eighty pole fighters, I ought to be able to set out confidently, march straight down our street, get going right now. (*WW*, p. 49; p. 50)

Kingston's solution, from the vantage point of adulthood, is her writing. Textual vengeance becomes the retribution that Kingston chooses to take:

> The swordswoman and I are not so dissimilar. May my people understand the resemblance soon so that I can return to them. What we have in common are the words at our backs. The idioms for *revenge* are 'report a crime' and 'report to five families'. The reporting is the vengeance – not the beheading, not the gutting, but the words. (*WW*, p. 53)

'Shaman', the third section of the novel, deals with Brave Orchid's life. As a pioneering doctor and scholar in China, war medic, vanquisher of ghosts, emancipator of Chinese girl slaves, expert and adventurous cook, competent mother and tireless labourer in her laundry in America, Brave Orchid herself functions as a model of female strength and accomplishment, and as an admirable survivor in her daughter's imagination. As Kingston sharply contrasts the mythical woman warrior's victories with her own 'voice unreliable' attempts to shout down the 'stupid racists', so she distinguishes between her mother's valiant deeds and her 'slum grubby' existence as an immigrant in America (*WW*, p. 50; p. 52). Brave Orchid's life is doubly textualised. The narrator herself pieces together her mother's history by sifting through the textual fragments that she discovers: Brave Orchid's medical diploma, graduation photographs and photographs of her father. Although this material is partly supplemented by Brave Orchid's stories about her life, the narrator is left to imaginatively reconstruct the missing sections of her mother's life. In fact, all of the narrator's experiences of China, including mythical narratives, are mediated textually; even her knowledge of her relatives and ancestors in China is gleaned from letters to her parents.

The fourth section, 'At the Western Palace', continues the narrator's exploration of her mother's life, but shifts the focus to America. We are introduced to the narrator's aunt, Moon Orchid, who comes to stay with her sister. As the complete antithesis of her sister, Moon Orchid is a frail and anxious woman, with little personality of her own. Once ensconced in her sister's house, she takes to trailing after her nephews and nieces (the narrator included), and verbally echoing their actions and movements. Moon Orchid's flimsy appearance and frailty of personality are reflected in the arrival gift that she presents to Maxine: a paper cutout of Fa Mu Lan. Whereas her sister gives the young girl tangible role models to which to aspire, Moon Orchid is able only to offer fragile paper figures. This inefficacy continues when Moon Orchid fails to live up to her sister's expectations of her existence in America, and slides into insanity. As many commentators have observed, Moon Orchid thus finally comes to reflect the 'lunacy' of her name.

The final section, 'A Song for a Barbarian Reed Pipe', unites the previous sections, weaving together the narratives of mother and daughter. In so doing, this section extensively interrogates the problems and paradoxes of the mother–daughter nexus. This is particularly apparent in relation to a speech-silence dichotomy. Kingston has already charted the narrator's ambivalence and occasional hostility towards her mother tongue, as well as her attempts to try to escape it. Frequently the site of a repressive representation of women (who are called 'slaves', 'maggots' and 'cowbirds' amongst other derogatory labels in the text), her move to escape Chinese as the language of repression and turn to English as the language of individualism runs parallel to her attempt to free herself from what she regards as a stifling maternal influence. Partly this desire for dissociation from the mother tongue is due to the embarrassment she feels at her parents' lack of accomplishment in English. For the narrator, her mother's poor English amplifies her humiliation at school: her own taciturnity causes her teachers to seek parental involvement, only to discover that 'my parents did not understand English' (*WW*, p. 149). The young Maxine's hostility also results from Brave Orchid's attempts to press her language knowledge into profitable service. Repeatedly, Maxine's humiliation is accentuated by her mother's insistence that she act as translator. As Kingston notes: 'You can't entrust your voice to the Chinese, either; they want to capture your voice for their own use. They want to fix up your tongue to speak for them. "How much less can you sell it for?" we have to say' (*WW*, p. 152). Yet for the young girl, this maternal pressure paradoxically results in silencing or mangling her speech. Brave Orchid's instructions, 'You just translate', preclude the young girl from doing so effectively, and her speech becomes warped.

Gradually, the young Maxine moves away from regarding Brave Orchid and her language as negative. This trajectory is engendered by a recognition on the daughter's part that her mother's language is actually more similar to her own than she had realised. Maxine's realisation is that the mother tongue is not actually Chinese; rather it is a mixture of Chinese and American, and it is this mixed, hybrid discourse that becomes the language of mother–daughter communication. A recognition of this shared lexicon, and the decision to speak – and of course later to write – completes the move towards resolution between mother and daughter, so that ending her text, Kingston is able to say, 'it translated well' (*WW*, p. 186).

The young girl's inability to converse confidently in English is also linked to a crisis of selfhood. She tells us: 'I could not understand "I". The Chinese "I" has seven strokes, intricacies. How could the American "I", assuredly wearing a hat like the Chinese, have only three strokes, the middle so straight?' (*WW*, p. 150). Maxine's taciturnity is thus bound to her struggle to reconcile conflicting Chinese and American cultural inheritances. Her resolution is not to collapse these dualities and contradictions, but instead to accommodate them in all of their complexity, and is highlighted in the final story that Maxine relates – one befittingly originally told to her by her mother – that of the singing poetess, Ts'ai Yen. A real historical figure, Ts'ai Yen lived in AD 175, the daughter of a scholar. She was captured and made to live in 'barbarian' lands for twelve years. She composed the long poem, 'Eighteen Stanzas for a Barbarian Reed Pipe', based upon her time in captivity, from which the final section of Kingston's work takes its title. As with her other uses of Chinese myths, Kingston has edited and changed this one to fit her purpose. Most notably, the Ts'ai Yen story emphasises that those estranged from an ancestral country will retain a psychological link with that culture, but also, more crucially, that this separation can be harnessed for creative purposes, as Ts'ai Yen did, and as Kingston does too. The Ts'ai Yen story is narrated by both mother and daughter, as Kingston famously tells us: 'The beginning is hers, the ending, mine' (*WW*, p. 184). At this point, stories and identities merge, so that Kingston as daughter contributes to her mother's text and vice-versa.

In her study of adolescent fiction, *Growing Up Female*, Barbara A. White defines the adolescent story as a version of 'the initiation story where the protagonist experiences a significant change of knowledge or character', and in which the central character 'rejects the constraints of home, sets out on a journey through the world, obtains guides who represent world views' and that figures 'estrangement from the social environment, conflict with parents, disillusionment in love, departure from home, and encounters with different people and ideas'.[20] The overwhelming critical emphasis upon feminist themes in *The Woman Warrior* has not only excised from view its inter-dependency in theme and subject with its companion volume *China Men*, as Maureen Sabine has lamented, but it has also obscured the central significance of the adolescent perspective in Maxine's story. Reading the text somewhat against the grain of its feminist plot, though, enables Maxine's story to emerge as a quintessential coming-of-age narrative that corresponds almost exactly to the plot and theme schema identified in White's study. The young Maxine rejects both the domestic confine-ment of home and the social constraints of her society in the manner suggested by White, and also garners female role models, such as Fa Mu Lan, to aid her journey to mature womanhood. White also identifies a host of recurrent themes in adolescent stories, many of which will be familiar to readers of *The Woman Warrior*: 'girls envy their brothers ... they express outrage at being molested by a man ... they try to avoid doing housework ... they say they feel enclosed, imprisoned, stuffed in a sack, or under a bell jar'; 'the protagonist is in conflict over her gender identity ... she rejects the traditional roles and vocations of women, especially marriage'; adolescent stories are 'characterized by conflict' and the adolescent must 'seek experi-ence in a conscious attempt to cultivate inner powers ... must question whatever values prevail in the society and construct her own morality and philosophy of life from the bottom up'.[21] Even more specifically, some of the key scenes in *The Woman Warrior* that I have described already, conform to common traits in adolescent girls' stories. A notable example is the young girl's struggle to reconcile conflicting maternal messages and to identify appropriate female role models who will bolster rather than batter the girl's fledgling self image. White observes that although 'Adolescent heroines would no doubt find it easier to grow up female if they could admire and identify with adult women', many 'have little opportunity to see any women other than their own mothers and neighbouring wives and mothers', so that

It is obviously a formidable task for girls to try to reject the female roles offered them and at the same time prove they can live up to these roles. They are reduced to striving to be 'feminine' and 'non-feminine' simultaneously;[22]

a description that is strikingly reminiscent of the young Maxine's efforts to reconcile the many conflicting messages and role models with which she is presented, and her struggles on the one hand to make herself 'American-pretty so that the five or six Chinese boys in the class fell in love with me, everyone else – the Caucasian, Negro, and Japanese boys – would too', whilst on the other, to go 'away to college – Berkeley in the sixties – and I studied, and I marched to save the world' (*WW*, p. 49). This ambivalence of perspective extends to a personal ambivalence on the part of the adolescent girl towards her mother, Brave Orchid; as White notes: 'The desire to champion the mother remains as strong as the impulse to deny her'.[23]

Maxine's freedom and maturity come via her imagination as she first dreams, then writes, her way to a strong, autonomous womanhood, a position in which she could combat oppression and victimisation:

To avenge my family, I'd have to storm across China to take back our farm from the Communists; I'd have to rage across the United States to take back the laundry in New York and the one in California. Nobody in history had conquered and united both North America and Asia. A descendant of eighty pole fighters, I ought to be able to set out confidently, march straight down our street, get going right now. (*WW*, p. 50)

This, too, is a common path:

Girls have fantasies of leaving home, travelling around the world, becoming famous writers or actresses, even of protesting the efforts of parents or suitors to control their behaviour;[24]

and it should be noted that it is also her mother who brokers this connection with a world of possibility, as Maxine remembers: 'I couldn't tell where the stories left off and the dreams began, her voice the voice of the heroines in my sleep' (*WW*, p. 25).

In her analysis, Barbara White reads a range of adolescent stories dating from the 1920s to the 1970s and the constancy of theme and perspective is quite remarkable. One of her examples is a short 1938 novel by Katherine Anne Porter, entitled *Old Mortality*, which bears a noteworthy resemblance to *The Woman Warrior* in plot, to the extent that it serves to highlight the convergence of perspective between the genre of adolescent writing and Kingston's own text. The central female character is a young girl called Miranda who is forced to reconstruct her disgraced deceased aunt's biography, only to discover that it was her unhappiness that led to an early death. Miranda re-reads this story as a tale of rebellion, for her own purposes, and this story is juxtaposed with her other aunt, Eva's, competence and ebullience, as a Latin teacher and suffragist, who is admired by Miranda for her combat against oppression and for championing the cause of women. The story reminds us of Maxine's confusion regarding the characteristics of her female forbears: her drowned-in-the-well aunt, frail aunt Moon Orchid and her formidable mother Brave Orchid, as well as her fervent attempts to reconstruct and interpret her deceased aunt's life story. In her key 1977 essay, 'The Feminist Novel of Androgynous Fantasy', Ellen Morgan identified 'at the heart of the feminist impulse ... a fierce hunger for images of authentic female selfhood – images which might illuminate what a liberated female person would be like';[25] in both *The Woman Warrior* and in Katherine Anne Porter's novel, we witness the necessity for both inspirational female relatives and the desperate attempt to recuperate the 'fallen' woman in the family as part of the adolescent girl's project of maturation.

The Woman Warrior as life writing

Maureen Sabine proposes that the young Maxine's project is 'to figure out the women's life histories'.[26] I see *The Woman*

Warrior's project as more than this; in fact I would suggest that the text itself encompasses an entire submerged signifying system that centres upon the female life cycle. Time in the text is measured by the menarchal–parturition cycle, as the young Maxine tells her mother:

> 'Time is not the same from place to place,' I said unfeelingly. 'There is only the eternal present, and biology. The reason you feel time pushing is that you had six children after you were forty-five and you worried about raising us.' (*WW*, p. 98)

The narrative can thus be tracked through parturition (the No Name Aunt), the menarche (the no name aunt's story is triggered by the young Maxine's onset of menstruation), and the post-partum connectivity that develops through the narrative between mother and daughter. Furthermore, the narrative is replete with images of menstruation as a time of psychological as well as actual fertility: Fa Mu Lan declares that 'Menstrual days did not interrupt my training: I was as strong as on any other day' (*WW*, p. 35) and the young Kingston notes 'as when a woman gives birth … I menstruated and dreamed red dreams' (*WW*, p. 38); menstruation is figured as a time for pensiveness: 'I bled and thought about the people to be killed; I bled and thought about the people to be born' (*WW*, p. 37); and the parturient woman is presented as inhabiting a heightened state of female strength and possibility, as Fa Mu Lan declares: 'Marriage and childbirth strengthen the swordswoman' (*WW*, p. 49). Uterine (inter)connectivity maps onto psychological intimacy amongst the women of the text; Brave Orchid trained in gynaecology and shamanism at the To Keung School of Midwifery, where she learned not just a profession but the life skill of independence: 'The students at the To Keung School of Midwifery were new women, scientists who changed the rituals' (*WW*, p. 72); and Brave Orchid is at the centre of the narrative as an actual and metaphorical midwife, reminding us that the term 'midwife' itself carries the meaning of 'the one who is with the mother'.

The sexual life cycle thus functions as a structuring device, but is also figured as a dangerous process for the young adolescent facing her sexuality for the first time. The menarche is often paradoxically heralded as a start of sexual adulthood yet also carries with it connotations of entering new, perilous territory. The young Maxine is all too aware of this and knowingly remarks that 'women at sex hazarded birth and hence lifetimes' (*WW*, p. 14). The menarche is also figured by Brave Orchid as a danger, as Maureen Sabine observes: 'Rather than explain that bleeding is a natural monthly occurrence, Brave Orchid shrouds the whole subject in the taboos of the after life and afterbirth'.[27] Consistently in the narrative, Brave Orchid encodes the female life cycle in her treatment of her daughter, as the narrator observes: 'No one talked sex, ever' (*WW*, p. 14), and when Brave Orchid does speak of sex, it is as a threat: 'Now that you have started to menstruate, what happened to her could happen to you' (*WW*, p. 13), she warns her daughter.

The most extensive – and extended – instance of sex-as-danger is the handling of the no name woman's story at the start of Maxine's narrative. Barbara White suggests that a notable change in adolescent stories as a result of the advent of second-wave feminism is an increased attention to subjects of concern to feminism, such as the mother–daughter relationship and the issue of rape and sexual violence.[28] In the light of this, it is significant that a tale of sexual downfall opens Kingston's adolescent story, and provides the context in which the young Maxine's struggle to define her sexual and gender identity takes place. Maxine's own reading of her aunt's tale of shame is resolutely in the context of sexual violence, and what she does not know, she imagines:

> My aunt could not have been the lone romantic who gave up everything for sex. Women in the old China did not choose. Some man had commanded her to lie with him and be his secret evil. I wonder whether he masked himself when he joined the raid on her family … And she might have separated the rapes from the rest of living if only she did not have to buy her oil from him or gather wood in the

same forest. I want her fear to have lasted just as long as the rape lasted so that the fear could have been contained. No drawn-out fear. (*WW*, p. 14)

The adult Kingston is also careful to retell the no name aunt's story in a manner that bears testimony to the trauma she must have suffered. There is a particular emphasis, for instance, upon the enormity, the physicality and the emotional intensity of the no name woman's ordeal – the physical pain:

When she felt the birth coming, she thought that she had been hurt. Her body seized together. 'They've hurt me too much,' she thought. 'This is gall, and it will kill me.' Her forehead and knees against the earth, her body convulsed and then released her onto her back; (*WW*, p. 20)

the psychological anguish:

Flayed, unprotected against space, she felt pain return, focusing her body. This pain chilled her – a cold, steady kind of surface pain. Inside, spasmodically, the other pain, the pain of the child, heated her. For hours she lay on the ground, alternately body and space; (*WW*, p. 20)

the intimacy of her connection with her newborn:

She reached down to touch the hot, wet, moving mass, surely smaller than anything human, and could feel that it was human after all – fingers, toes, nails, nose. She pulled it up onto her belly, and it lay curled there ... She opened her loose shirt and buttoned the child inside. After resting, it squirmed and thrashed and she pushed it up to her breast. It turned its head this way and that until it found her nipple. There, it made little snuffling noises. She clenched her teeth at its preciousness; (*WW*, p. 21)

her psychological and physical isolation:

She ran out into the fields, far enough from the house so that she could no longer hear their voices; (*WW*, p. 20)

and finally, the unbearable act of killing herself and her child:

Full of milk, the little ghost slept. When it awoke, she hardened her breasts against the milk that crying loosens.

Towards morning she picked up the baby and walked to
the well. (*WW*, p. 21)

Kingston's mature rendering of her aunt's story from an overtly
emotive, physical and feminist perspective, and her subsequent
identification with her aunt's tragic predicament, extensively
imbricates her own life story with her aunt's, to the extent that
Maureen Sabine suggests that Kingston's life writing itself
becomes 'an incestuous narrative activity'.[29] Not surprisingly
then, this tale of sexual woe is enough to scare the young girl,
who notes that 'my aunt haunts me' (*WW*, p. 21) and who later
declares that 'I'm never getting married, never!' (*WW*, p. 180).
Barbara White observes that cautionary tales such as the no
name woman story often serve to put young girls off sex:

> many adolescent heroines associate sexual intercourse with
> male domination … almost every aspect of sex reminds
> adolescent heroines of a future they dread … intercourse
> suggests to them domination and exploitation by men,
> menarche curtailment of their activity, childbearing,
> severe pain and a restricted role.[30]

As a 'story to grow up on' (*WW*, p. 13), as Kingston puts it, the
no name woman fable's placement at the outset of Kingston's
narrative thereby sets a somewhat bleak tone for the rest of the
book.

Kingston's reconstruction of her aunt's story – her search
for what could be called her aunt's 'life traces' – metaphorically
brings her aunt back to life, since the record of life itself is
rendered as memory; as Maxine notes: 'the real punishment was
… deliberately forgetting her' (*WW*, p. 22). The no name
woman's story thus literally and figuratively opens the family
archives, and the investigation of family history that is thereby
triggered becomes the young Kingston's ongoing endeavour. In
her book *The Voice of the Mother: Embedded Maternal Narratives in Twentieth-Century Women's Autobiographies* (2000),
Jo Malin observes that 'many twentieth-century autobiographical texts by women contain an intertext, an embedded narrative,
which is a biography of the writer/daughter's mother'.[31] Malin

explores the manner in which the stories of mother and daughter 'overlap, and the mother, the object of the biographical narrative, becomes a subject, or rather an "intersubject", in her daughter's autobiography'.[32] Malin does not include *The Woman Warrior* in her discussion, possibly due to its hazy generic status, yet Kingston's work coincides exactly with this description of women's intersubjective life-writing practice. Malin suggests that this process/practice becomes a form of feminist *praxis* in women's life writing, one that seeks to resist the use of a mono-logic, authoritative narrative voice, in preference for a form of intersubjective conversational inscription:

> These daughters are not simply telling their mothers' stories. They are engaged in conversation. … a hybrid form of autobiographical narrative containing an embedded narrative of the mother; the daughter/writer as a subject attempts to speak to her mother as a subject rather than about her as an object.[33]

Thus, women's feminist life-writing praxis comes to mirror women's conversational *practices*, as a form of group identifi-cation and affirmation. Malin's ideas here also mirror Rita Felski's influential formulation of feminist confessional practices in her study, *Beyond Feminist Aesthetics* (1989).[34] Felski identi-fies feminist confession as a narrative or life-writing mode of expression that not only emphasises, but also valorises, private female discourse; and furthermore, it provides an apposite mode for the (re)telling of the traditionally private, everyday, sometimes painful, exclusive experiences of women. Of feminist confession, Jo Malin writes:

> Feminist confession tends to emphasize the more private and everyday experiences of women, which can also be 'traumatic,' such as domestic violence or pregnancy 'scares.' These narratives often include descriptions of physical details of female bodies that 'bind women together.' Thus a communal identity rather than an emphasis on individual traits predominates in such texts. … These texts also include the reader in an intimacy that assumes a sharing of common experiences, many of which are sited in the body.[35]

Two theorists of women's life writing, Sidonie Smith and Julia Watson, have recently characterised the form of female life writing itself as imbricated in an embodied politics of remembering, as 'an activity situated in cultural politics … a collective activity', reminding us that as subjects 'we move in and out of various communities of memory – religious, racial, ethnic, familial'.[36] I would like to suggest that *The Woman Warrior* works as a kind of feminist life-writing 'confession by proxy', in so far as the mature Kingston refigures and re-imagines the biographies of those women who form her psychological and subjective community: the no name aunt, Fa Mu Lan, Brave Orchid, Moon Orchid, and finally Ts'ai Yen. Furthermore, this confessional practice functions by way of an especially embodied narrative mode, since as Smith and Watson remind us, women's 'life narrative inextricably links memory, subjectivity, and the materiality of the body'.[37] Smith and Watson add that

> By exploring the body and embodiment as sites of knowledge and knowledge production, life narrations … engage, contest, and revise cultural norms determining the relationship of bodies to specific sites, behaviours, and destinies;[38]

suggesting the extent to which it is only by way of an identification with the embodied experience of the shamed no name aunt that Kingston can gain access to her story and stage its retelling from an oppositional perspective in the text. Since the narrative opens with this formative fable, the pattern is thus set for Kingston's retelling of her own story and the interconnected stories of the other female figures. Women's body processes and practices – menstruation, sexual intercourse, childbirth, post-parturience – thereby take on added significance in the text as a form of memory access and retrieval itself. Thus, the narrative becomes what Smith and Watson name 'scriptotherapy' – the struggle to tell, and understand, women's traumatic, embodied, experience.[39]

In *Women Writing Childbirth*, Tess Cosslett has researched women's revision of prescriptive versions of the childbirth story from their own perspectives, across a range of genres, from the fictional to the auto/biographical. Cosslett finds a remarkable consistency in the process whereby women seek to narrate childbirth for themselves. Noting that traditionally 'childbirth did not appear' in narrative 'and when it did it was nearly always seen from an audience point of view', and that 'accounts of childbirth from the perspective of the birthing woman herself have been relegated to private diaries', Cosslett searches for examples in which the birthing woman tells her own story.[40] She finds a process in which the consciousness of the birthing woman struggles with 'the power to take over the story' *and* 'the power to control the experience'.[41] Kingston's retelling of her no name aunt's story reflects this dual struggle, whereby Kingston endeavours to wrest the meaning of the tale from its association with patriarchal and traditional cultural suppression and prohibition in favour of a more resolutely positive interpretation. Through this recuperation, Kingston also participates in what Cosslett calls 'the oral tradition of women telling each other about childbirth'.[42] Cosslett views this as an oppositional female practice, whereby women are able to bypass official 'meanings' of childbirth. Kingston's account takes place in a slightly different context, since the circumstances of the original telling occurred when it was relayed to the young girl as a warning; yet retold by Kingston as a fable of resistance, it is transformed into the potentially oppositional 'myth of birth' that Cosslett identifies.[43] Kingston has described this revision:

> It wasn't me that started breaking the silence about the 'no name woman.' My mother did it; she's the first one that said, 'Let's remember this story.' And actually she's even the one who gave it a meaning, but then her meaning was just don't fool around or you're going to get pregnant and get in big trouble. But she broke the frozen ice. Then the struggle on my part was to say no to that meaning.[44]

Although the no name woman does not – indeed cannot – relate her own tale, Kingston stands in for her as an assertive substitute female subjectivity, and via the processes of embodied identification that I have explored, Kingston and her aunt meld perspectives, so much so that they in effect become kin subjectivities.[45]

Talk-story and other forms

> At last I saw that I too had been in the presence of great
> power, my mother talking-story. (*The Woman Warrior*,
> p. 25)

As I have discussed, the mode of discourse in *The Woman
Warrior* is a form of woman-to-woman intimacy, a telling and
(re)telling that steps back and forth across the line that divides
public and private, subjectivity and intersubjective liaison.
Kingston conceives of this as an ethnic-specific mode, that of
'talk-story'. We may also conceive of talk-story in *The Woman
Warrior* as a form of feminist praxis, in the manner that I have
outlined above. In *The Life Writing of Otherness*, Lauren Rusk
observes that 'Kingston's talk-stories bespeak a female collec-
tivity', and views the form of talk-story as 'artistic product ... a
work both collective and singular – a singular interpretation of
that which has been collectively imagined'.[46] The talk-story
form therefore enables Kingston to gather together the divergent stories of female kith and kin under the umbrella of her
own exploration of female selfhood and subjectivity. As 'memoirs',
her narrative enables a loosely arranged and roughly assembled
series of reminiscences and stories – talk-stories – to come
together. Rusk notes that the form of her text allows Kingston a
flexibility and inclusiveness of style that she would not otherwise possess. Sidonie Smith and Julia Watson define the memoir as

> A mode of life narrative that historically situates the
> subject in a social environment, as either observer or
> participant; the memoir directs attention more toward the
> lives and actions of others than to the narrator;[47]

and suggest that whereas the 'I' of autobiography is by and large
singular, the 'I' of memoir is often dialogic, externalised or
collective. Kingston's 'I's include all of the actual as well as
mythical female figures that she allows to take central stage in
the story, to the extent that at times the figure of Kingston
herself disappears from view. In fact, Rusk observes that whilst
the memoir is ostensibly Kingston's own, 'the text enables us to

visualize Brave Orchid more clearly than it does her daughter'.[48]

Many feminist critics of Kingston's work have attributed her use of talk-story to her feminist politics. Wendy Ho's discussion in *In Her Mother's House: The Politics of Asian American Mother–Daughter Writing*, describes the role of talk-story in *The Woman Warrior*:

> Her cultural text testifies to the complicated task of constructing a self talking-story that re-envisions and enacts a more transformative social and political subjectivity in the face of considerable psychosocial, as well as cultural and historical, disorientation, violence, and loss.[49]

Ho sees the process of talk-story itself as the means of retrieval of women's sometimes buried, often embodied stories:

> talk-stories often come by necessity with a complicated vocabulary of rupture … the 'dis-ease' of the great unsaids. To understand this nuanced language of embodied feeling is to develop a level of sensitivity and patience for the details in the developing patterns of love and intimacy that structure intricate relationships and identifications.[50]

So for Ho, to listen to talk-story is to learn to be a code-breaker, to decipher the intricate and subtle nuances of embodied feeling in signifiers. In another feminist interpretation, King-kok Cheung observes that Kingston's 'recourse to talk-story – which blurs the distinction between straight facts and pure fiction – accomplishes two key objectives: to reclaim a past and, more decisively, to envision a different future'.[51] Talk-story enables Kingston to shift subject or emphasis both structurally and thematically at any moment in the text and thereby to gain access to different stories, sometimes simultaneously. Although Ho, Cheung, and I, have designated it as a feminist, as well as ethnic, strategy, we should remember that the talk-story technique is one that Kingston also employed in *China Men*, which, we recall, was initially conceived as part of the same story as *The Woman Warrior*. The separation of the one originally planned book into two, occurred late in the writing process. In her 'Statement of Plans', Kingston wrote:

I had planned an enormous opus incorporating both books, but *The Woman Warrior* seemed to break itself away naturally from the rest of the chapters probably because of its strong feminist viewpoint. Some of the 'hero' chapters undermined this viewpoint. This separation of the stories about the women and the stories about the men is an accurate artistic form for telling the history of Chinese Americans. ... *The Woman Warrior* was about a matriarchal tradition.[52]

Kingston said that 'to write true stories of the lives of people who have powerful imaginations and dreams, I needed to record exactly what their dreams and visions are. I come from a culture and family in which we know one another by knowing one another's dreams and visions. The process is talk story.'[53] Ultimately, for Kingston, the talk-story form becomes a new kind of genre, one malleable to her own purposes:

I am open to hearing talk-story. It's part of my culture. This is what my family does. I hope you see that talk-story actually reverberates. These stories don't end, they didn't have a beginning. I just wrote down parts of them. In talk-story, every time you tell a story it changes, it grows.[54]

China Men (1980)

Chinese American history is a history of separation; there was a women's culture of waiting in China and a men's culture – Chinaman in America. (Maxine Hong Kingston, 'The Gold Mountain Man')[1]

When I say I am a native American with all the rights of an American, I am saying, 'No, we're not outsiders; we Chinese belong here. This is our country, this is our history, we are a part of America. If it weren't for us, America would be a different place'. (Maxine Hong Kingston, Interview with Marilyn Yalom)[2]

Gold mountain heroes

The original title of Maxine Hong Kingston's second book was not 'China Men' but 'Gold Mountain Heroes'. Kingston's decision to call her first draft by this name was linked to her desire to tell her male and female ancestors' stories separately, because 'The Woman Warrior seemed to break itself away naturally from the rest of the chapters probably because of its strong feminist viewpoint. Some of the "hero" chapters undermined this viewpoint'.[3] This might suggest that the material that comprised China Men constituted the leftovers from the mythic-psychic feast that was The Woman Warrior; yet as Kingston has explained, her division of these hi/stories along gender lines actually reflects the emergence of each gender story:

This separation of the stories about the women and the stories about the men is an accurate artistic form for telling the history of Chinese Americans. The patterns of migration, especially as influenced by the Chinese Exclusion Acts, effectively separated Chinese American men from their wives for about 70 years (from 1882 until 1952 when Chinese women were allowed to immigrate on the same bases as men). The Chinatowns have been bachelor societies. THE WOMAN WARRIOR was about a matriarchal tradition; GOLD MOUNTAIN HEROES is about a patriarchal tradition.[4]

Although Kingston was to discard the title 'Gold Mountain Heroes' in a later draft, her original use signals her intention to create a history of her Chinese American male ancestors that both mythologised and celebrated their arrival in America, a place Chinese immigrants named 'Gold Mountain'; and to commemorate their efforts to bond with their new land and country, and the hard labour they undertook in these endeavours. In 1986 Kingston told interviewer Paula Rabinowitz that in this project she also meant to evoke the work of two literary predecessors:

I am creating part of American literature ... I directly continue William Carlos Williams' *In the American Grain.* He stopped in 1860 and I pick it up in 1860 and carry it forward. ... I use the title 'The Making of More Americans,' from Gertrude Stein, because when I read *The Making of Americans,* I thought, 'Yes, she is creating a language that is the American language; and she is doing it sentence by sentence. I am trying to write an American language that has Chinese accents'.[5]

William Carlos Williams is especially important to Kingston as a role model because, as she explains, 'he tells the story of America as myth ... and I wanted to do American history in the same way ... I pick up when the Chinese Americans came, and I showed how the Chinese made the bands of steel, which is a railroad, and they banded the country back together again.'[6] As many commentators have observed, Kingston's project in *China*

Men therefore, made more manifest in this book than in *The Woman Warrior*, is what Maureen Sabine refers to as the 'restoration of the male descent line', the insertion into historical discourse and popular imaginative record of the story of the Chinese American pioneers of the nineteenth and twentieth centuries.[7]

Kingston tells this story in six roughly chronological chapters, which span the mid-nineteenth century (the first wave of Chinese American immigration and their role in the construction of the transcontinental railroad) to the mid-twentieth century (the conscription of soldiers for the Vietnam conflict). In addition to each chapter's historical emphasis, each connects with other sections via interlinking thematic preoccupations or characters that appear more than once. These chapters are then punctuated by a series of retold Chinese myths. Thus, Kingston is deliberately echoing the form of *The Woman Warrior*. She has explained this in detail:

> The form of GOLD MOUNTAIN HEROES will be as close as I can make it to THE WOMAN WARRIOR. I am calling the form 'biographical novel,' an experimentation with a way to tell the story of a culture of story-tellers. The characters tell stories about one another, and also about the Chinese past and mythology and the new Chinese American legends. Stylistically, I am discovering the Chinese American voice, which is American English influenced by Chinese rhythms, attitudes and images. It is particularly satisfying to use Chinese American vocabulary and syntax and to describe the world from the viewpoints of people who think in a combination of modern American English and Chinese speech and ideographs. There is an amalgam, a new American rhythm. In THE WOMAN WARRIOR, there are five stories which are distinct but related in themes and characters. In GOLD MOUNTAIN HEROES, there are six such stories. Between each of the six stories are mythical, archetypal stories.[8]

The first story, 'The Father from China', is told from the young Maxine's perspective, and tracks her struggle to discover her father's history – specifically, the means by which he emigrated to the United States. This confusion is reflected in the

proliferation of versions of her father's history which are told to
the young girl: as Kingston has rather gleefully observed in
interviews, 'In the course of the book, I have him coming into
this country in five different ways. I'm very proud of that.'⁹ The
existence of conflicting versions of these stories is also more
than simply a reflection of the adolescent Maxine's uncertainty
though; in *China Men* as in *The Woman Warrior* it becomes a
literary technique, part of Kingston's mixed-genre style, as
Kingston explains in relation to 'The Father from China':

> immigration is told in two contradicting and intersecting
> stories, a technique I pulled off in Chapter 1 of THE
> WOMAN WARRIOR. He either stowed away on a ship
> from Cuba, or he passed the immigration tests at Angel
> Island. The last half of the chapter shows the utter joy of
> America – a surprising discovery. I have included trans-
> lations of writings by the Chinamen, as they called them-
> selves; these were celebrations and laments about their life
> in the West, and are, I suppose, part of American literature
> though written in Chinese.[10]

Kingston's second chapter shifts focus from the continental
United States to consider another significant immigration route
for early Chinese Americans: to Hawai'i, in 'The Great Grandfather of the Sandalwood Mountains'. Here the two great-
grandfathers work on a sugar cane plantation in the 1850s, a
common occupation for early Chinese immigrants to Hawai'i.
Kingston documents both the hardships and the racism these
men endured, including the white plantation overseers' tax against
talking, and the difficulties the Chinese immigrants experienced
in trying the relocate to the mainland U.S. The following
section, 'The Grandfather of the Sierra Nevada Mountains',
works together with the Hawai'i section in recording the lives
and livelihoods of the Chinese immigrants on the mainland in
the 1850s and 1860s (the transcontinental railroad was
completed in 1869). Here we find the 'railroad grandfather',
whose task it is to hack away at the Sierra granite to carve a
space for the Central Pacific Transcontinental Railroad to pass
from west to east. Several themes from the preceding section

provide continuity between the two chapters. The image of fire that was introduced via the burning of sugar cane in the Sandal-wood Mountains chapter, resurfaces here as dynamite explosions in the Sierra Nevada mountains. The plantation employers' aggression is echoed here in the railroad bosses' suppression of the Chinese American workers' strike for better pay and con-ditions. The most extensive connection, though, is between the meditations upon nature in which each Chinese American man engages, as a means of escaping the hardships of daily toil, and via the construction of an imaginative engagement with his sur-roundings. As I discuss in the chapter on Kingston's book *Hawai'i One Summer*, in her work Kingston often uses an emotional engagement with the environment as a means of expressing a sense of both belonging and ownership. In both the Hawai'i and Sierra Nevada sections of *China Men*, we find extensive meditations upon the wonders of nature and the universe. The China men exhibit a heightened connection with their surround-ings, as the following quotation from 'The Great Grandfather of the Sandalwood Mountains' chapter serves to illustrate:

> He sucked in deep breaths of the Sandalwood Mountain air, and let it out in a song, which reached up to the rims of volcanoes and down to the edge of the water. His song lifted and fell with the air, which seemed to breathe warmly through his body and through the rocks. The clouds and frigate birds made the currents visible, and the leaves were loud. If he did not walk heavy seated and heavy thighed like a warrior, he would float away, snuggle into the wind, and let it slide him down to the ocean, let it make a kite, a frigate bird, a butterfly of him.[11]

In this section, Kingston unusually appears briefly as an adult commentator on her relative's Hawai'i days, and figures her own close connection with this place too, in a five paragraph medita-tion upon the landscape of Hawai'i. The final lines explicitly connect nature and 'Americanisation':

> I have heard the land sing. I have seen the bright blue streaks of spirits whisking through the air. I again search for my American ancestors by listening in the air. (*CM*, p. 92)

Likewise, in the Sierra Nevada chapter, we see Ah Goong's bond with his environment:

> During the day he watched the magpies, big black and white birds with round bodies like balls with wings; they were a welcome sight, a promise of meetings. He had found two familiars in the wilderness: magpies and stars. (*CM*, p. 130)

Later in this chapter, I will explore Kingston's complex negotiation of, and claim to, a sense of an American identity; here we witness her claim by means of a land/person connectivity, a technique that is repeatedly recycled in the Hawai'i section of the book.

The next piece, 'The Making of More Americans', explicitly echoes the title of Gertrude Stein's book, *The Making of Americans* (1925). The books have many parallels: a focus upon the fortunes of immigrants, as representative of the 'making of Americans'; a style of narrative digression into other concerns; a preoccupation with the nature of history and historical record; and perhaps most significantly, the provision of individual character's histories. In her 'Statement of Plans' for *China Men*, Kingston describes this as 'the pivotal chapter and is about Americans'. She elaborates upon her focus:

> Third and Fourth Grandfathers and how they lived and died in America, how the latter's ghost tries to remain here; 2) the ex-river pirate great uncle who appeared briefly in THE WOMAN WARRIOR, and how he makes his agonizing decision to stay in America; 3) Big Brother escorts his mother's ghost back to China and returns a free man to America; 4) the uncle who cures his paranoid-schizophrenia by returning to China a Communist; 5) the uncle who decides to be an American after flying back and forth. These five stories connect and make the point that we are Americans, and at last some of the characters admit it.[12]

As this quotation indicates, Kingston is also more consistently and fully present as a character in both this, and in the following chapter, as a close relative of all these Chinese American ancestors. She relates the story of Say Goong and Sahm Goong

(Third and Fourth Grandfathers), 'Mad Sao' (the Big Brother), Kau Goong (the ex-river pirate), Uncle Bun (the Communist uncle) and I Fu (Aunt's Husband), via her own reminiscences of each character and the family lore about each that she inherits by way of oft-told family stories.

Kingston's next historical section, 'The American Father', brings the story into the present of her own childhood, and the reminiscences she has of her own father, BaBa. Here too, versions of his story proliferate. One fact, though, is constant, and is stressed from the outset: her father is an American citizen, and we are now in the realm of the contemporary. Here is the opening:

> In 1903 my father was born in San Francisco, where my grandmother had come disguised as a man. Or, Chinese women once magical, she gave birth at a distance, she in China, my grandfather and father in San Francisco. She was good at sending. Or the men of those days had the power to have babies. If my grandparents did no such wonders, my father nevertheless turned up in San Francisco an American citizen. (*CM*, p. 231)

Although this section describes BaBa's life in detail – his family life and his job running a pigeon lottery gambling house – much of this history is told askance, and the section is notable for BaBa's strange silences and his reticence in engaging with his family.

The final piece chronicles Kingston's brother's experiences as a soldier conscripted in the Vietnam conflict, and thereby completes the text's journey from the 1860s to the 1960s. In her plans for the book, Kingston notes that she wanted the narrator to disappear in this chapter again, to allow for the viewpoint of the brother to dominate, a strategy intended to underscore both the conflicting allegiances with which he was faced, and his psychological turmoil as a 'Berkeley pacifist' forced to go to war: 'He has to decide whether to be drafted, to try for conscientious objector status, or to go to Canada. The Asian American going to fight in Asia is our worst nightmare' she observed.[13] Despite his evasive manoeuvres, he is sent to Vietnam, but he emerges unscathed, his principles intact, and most importantly, the 'one good thing he gets out of Vietnam is [the] confirmation that the family is really American', an apposite note on which to end the narrative.[14]

Genre, nationhood and belonging

In Kingston's rendition of the gamut of Chinese American men's experiences on Gold Mountain, literature, history, biography, cartography and law all figure as discourses producing ideas of nationhood. As I have explored, and Kingston has asserted, the text itself is at times literature, at others biography, memoir or history, or a mixture of several modes. Kingston's traversal of discursive boundaries is a strategy that effectively reveals the ways in which the authority of such discourses is employed to legitimate and fix images of the nation as an exclusive in-group. By exploring what it means to be an 'American', Kingston's text represents a new concept of literary history, as well as of nationhood, and demonstrates how concepts of 'American' and the American 'nation' signify a particular, exclusive cultural and geographical terrain. Through this, Kingston seeks to challenge notions of nationhood, citizenship, subjecthood, history and literature, in a way that attempts to claim both textual and physical territory for her ancestors.[15]

Fiction, Jeff Spinner tells us, is a battleground of both individual and collective identity.[16] Identity is negotiated in relation to the collective concept of the 'nation'. Narration can therefore be said to create the nation, which in turn defines the individual either as part of that nation or as an outsider. To use Benedict Anderson's definition, the nation is an imagined political community, with imagined boundaries and collective traits, and the location of these imaginings are the cultural arenas of literature, history and legislature, as well as other textual media.[17] Benedict Anderson's theory of nationhood has been elaborated by Homi Bhabha in his key essay 'DissemiNation', which links the production of nationalism to nation-making texts, in an attempt to make visible literature's function as a cultural producer as well as product of nationalist discourses and sentiments.[18] Implicit in this argument is the recognition that the nation is not fixed but evolving, not organic but inorganic, and that it does not correspond to actual, but rather to conceptual spatial and territorial boundaries. The boundaries of national membership – or more accurately non-membership – are inscribed in citizenship legislature, as well as public, economic and social structures and institutions. It is these legal and institutional sites, as well as cultural media like literary and historical texts, where battles over identity take place. *China Men* tells the story of the male Chinese immigrants' embattled quest for membership of the nation, to become Americans, citizens of the American state and the accompanying entitlement to ownership of the land. The ascription of national membership in the text of *China Men* means that it is not only the narrative that contests notions of nationhood and nationality, but the text itself claims its place as a nation-making text, revising and re-imagining the community of the American nation to take account of ethnic subjects and diaspora presences like the China men. Homi Bhabha writes that:

> counter narratives of the nation … continually evoke and erase its totalising boundaries – both actual and conceptual – disturb those ideological manoeuvres through which 'imagined communities' are given essentialist identities.[19]

China Men can thus be said to contest and disrupt the ideological manoeuvres of the nation-state that define the China men as outsiders of the imagined communities of 'America'.

In *China Men* Kingston utilises a range of forms of intertextual, intra-textual and extra-textual contestation. The text is an example of what Linda Hutcheon calls 'historiographic metafiction'[20] in terms of its theoretical and generic self-awareness and its project of rethinking and questioning the epistemological status of historical, geographical and theoretical discourses, as they are seen to participate in the production of nationalist ideologies. The problems of identifying the generic status of

Kingston's work are well documented,[21] in this book and elsewhere, and yet as I have observed, this traversal of generic
categories on Kingston's part is quite deliberate. Variously
described as 'history', 'fiction', 'memoir' or 'biography', *China
Men* encapsulates the on-going contest between different kinds
of narratives in order to highlight how our attempts to delimit
our cultural chronicles and stories produce epistemologically
deceptive versions of our realities. Kingston has written:

> The mainstream culture doesn't know the history of
> Chinese-Americans ... so all of a sudden, right in the
> middle of the stories, plunk – there is an eight-page section
> of pure history ... there are no characters in it. It really
> affects the shape of the book and it might look quite
> clumsy.[22]

Far from 'clumsy', to have 'pure history' embedded in the middle
of the stories masterminds a skilful confrontation between two
different discourses. The subjective, personal and fictionalised
histories of the China men in the text serve to challenge and
often to contradict the 'official' version of history to be found in
'The Laws' section. By way of this clash, official and non-official
versions of history co-exist in such a way that the 'pure history'
sections are exposed as a far from 'pure', uncontaminated version
of the past and are instead presented simply as a different way of
telling the same story, equally 'contaminated' by personal biases
and viewpoints. The juxtaposition of ostensibly very different
genres, history and fiction (one of which carries more epistemological authority than the other), serves to expose both the
precarious status of the 'truth claim' of history and the inherent
fictionality of historical discourse. Kingston's exposure of history
as an ideologically constructed and value-laden narrative, also
highlights history's role in the production of 'nation' as a
'unisonant'[23], rooted and legitimate entity through the recita-
tion of a genealogy of origins.

   History and fiction are not the only generic sites of contestation in the text. The authority of autobiography is treated with
equal mistrust. Here, too, the jostle between the traditionally

conflicting and very separate discourses of autobiography and fiction is enacted in the text, and the fictional versions of the China men's stories again question the averment of autobiographical 'truth'. Kingston continually emphasises how incomplete and often uncertain her knowledge of her grandfathers' stories is: 'Maybe that Grandfather's Citizenship Judge was real and legal after all' (*CM*, p. 291). She even questions her biographical subjects for information within the text: 'Did you cut your pigtail to show your support for the public? Or have you always been American?' (*CM*, p. 18). Since both autobiography and biography are narratives of genesis, Kingston's deployment of autobiographical discourse to tell the story of the China men's claim to America and to American nationality and citizenship, has ironic resonances for the genealogies of origins that she is concerned with questioning.

Kingston has another purpose in throwing the discourses of history, fiction, autobiography and biography into contestation with each other. The strategy of mixing generic media precludes the reader from reading the text monologically – as history *or* autobiography *or* fiction – and making corresponding assumptions about the referentiality of that discourse. This highlights the tendency to read all texts by 'ethnic' or 'minority' writers (whatever the *declared* generic status of the text) as being in some way representative.[24] Thus, multi-media texts like *China Men* resist interpretation as an authoritative version of that ethnic group's story. For example, Kingston tells the story of several 'grandfathers' in her text. Grandfathers become almost generic;[25] there are simply too many to be blood relatives, and each grandfather represents part of the wider Chinese American immigrant story: of the search for gold; of working on the railroad, or on a sugarcane farm, or setting up a laundry. Yet the strategy of presenting these stories as the biographies of her grandfathers allows Kingston to offer them as textual warnings against the conflation of all ethnic or minority subjects as other to a white readership.

This competition between fictional, historical and autobiographical discourses is further complicated by Kingston's manipulation of myth. *China Men* opens with a story about a man called Tang Ao, who went looking for the Gold Mountain, but instead found the 'Land of Women', where he underwent enforced feminisation through ear-piercing, epilation and footbinding. As Donald C. Goellnicht has pointed out, this myth has been adapted from the nineteenth-century Chinese novel *Flowers in the Mirror* by Li Ju-Chen.[26] Kingston has altered the myth to suit her own purposes, as she did in *The Woman Warrior*. She highlights the precarious nature of myth-as-history by offering two dates for this mythic story – in AD 694–705 or in AD 441. As 'The Laws' section forms the structural centre of the text, so this myth 'On Discovery' constitutes the beginning, signalling to the reader that myth should be accorded equal validity as a legitimate version of the past as history or autobiography or biography, discourses more commonly supposed to be grounded in 'fact'. Or, to read Kingston's purpose another way, she demonstrates the instability of *all* of these discourses as factual retrospectives, consistent with her belief that stories change each time they are told. Thus, in *China Men*, history, autobiography, biography, myth and fiction are all placed on a generic continuum.

The power of mythical fictions is also emphasised in the Lo Bun Sun mythical story. Intended as an auditory pun[27] on *Robinson Crusoe*, this story echoes Daniel Defoe's narrative, charting as it does the hero's journey to a deserted island, his struggle for survival and eventual establishment of a colony on the island. The purpose of including this myth is twofold. As with the previous examples, the myth is accorded equal weight with more factual narratives in terms of its potency and endurance as an inherited cultural tale. The Lo Bun Sun story also serves to interrogate and contest American myths of origins. Like *Robinson Crusoe*, the Lo Bun Sun story is a narrative of colonisation but here is both inverted and subverted, because the subject position of coloniser is inhabited by a Chinese, rather than a white, British man (Robinson Crusoe). Thus, in the story that Kingston relates, it is the non-white subject that inhabits the position of settler; in an ironic reversal of American myths of origins where it is the white man who civilises and colonises, and with regard to Chinese American history, in this mythical version it is the Chinese Americans rather than the Anglo Americans who arrive first. The use of the Lo Bun Sun story thus not only highlights the provisionality of narrative, but also becomes part of Kingston's wider project of (re)colonisation, to '(re)claim America',[28] as she puts it, for her male ancestors. This revision by a 'minority' writer of a dominant cultural myth of origin serves to disrupt claims by Anglo culture of supremacy and to question such a genealogy of origin. Kingston's rewriting of both the Tang Ao and the Lo Bun Sun myths, literally authorises competing versions of history in her text, as well as the Chinese American claim to America.

Territoriality and textuality

The way in which concepts of territory and territoriality meet textuality in *China Men*, constitutes an example of the kind of frontier literary history advocated by Annette Kolodny in her seminal essay 'Letting Go Our Grand Obsessions'.[29] Kolodny's vision of frontier literary history points to the duality of meaning in the word 'authorise'. To write history, she suggests, is to both inscribe ownership and to colonise (as in 'inhabit'). Kolodny emphasises that frontiers – cultural as well as geographical – are created out of the contestation of territory (again, cultural as well as geographical territory), or con*front*ation, so that cultural and geographical spaces are only defined in opposition to something: the presence of another culture, territory or interest group. She cites Howard Lamar and Leonard Thompson's definition of the frontier as 'a territory or zone of *inter*penetration between … previously distinct societies' (italics mine).[30] In Kolodny's model, the frontier is as much human as geographical, and results from human/cultural contestations: 'there always stands at the heart of frontier literature … a physical terrain that, for at least one group of participants, is newly encountered and is undergoing change because of that encounter'.[31] The frontier, then, is envisioned as an imagined boundary between nation and non-nation, so that a cultural group excluded from national membership would be forced, as is the case with the China men, to inhabit the border between nation and non-nation. Cultural confrontation can be enacted textually and therefore the texts – and the languages that those texts inscribe – themselves participate in this confrontation: 'the collisions and negotiations of distinct cultural groups as expressed "en el choque e interaccion" of languages and texts', as Kolodny describes it.[32] The frontier is therefore perceived as the result of a process of dialogic negotiation; Kolodny writes that it is 'a locus of first cultural contact ... my paradigm would thus have us interrogating language – especially as hybridised style, trope, story or structure – for the complex intersections of human encounters and human encounters with the physical environment'.[33] Consequently, frontier literary history as advocated by Kolodny documents an evolving rather than static frontier, and carries the recognition that the physical and cultural landscape is constantly revised in the face of new inhabitants and new presences. This is very different from the 'grand narrative of discovery and progress' eschewed by Kolodny, in which 'cultural narratives of frontier battles, discoveries and negotiations' are all conflated into one.[34] By way of this formulation, the frontier emerges as an imagined boundary, inscribed textually, and does not correspond to a fixed external reality; it is figured as a fictional rather than (f)actual construction. Kolodny also observes that the frontier has always been identified with personal, as well as political, gain.[35] The original expansion of the American frontier westwards, Kolodny writes, was facilitated by the lure of fertile land in California.[36] It is, therefore, a territory contested by personal as well as collective presences and interests and the possibilities for colonisation should therefore be seen in the context of personal greed or control as well as of national interests.

I would suggest that *China Men* is one such frontier literary history. The text is a historical, geographical, as well as literary palimpsest, that reflects the continually evolving territory of the

American West. *China Men* charts the cultural frontier contests between the already resident white Americans and the newly arrived China men, and the ways in which this contestation transmutes and transforms geographical and cultural frontiers. As Kolodny suggests that it is human encounters with each other and with the physical environment that create the frontier,[37] so *China Men* tells the story of the China men grandfathers' interactions with their new physical environment, both the mythologised Gold Mountain and the Sandalwood Mountains of Hawai'i. The China men working in the mines and on the railroad actually transform the physical environment: 'China men banded the nation North and South, East and West, with criss-crossing steel. They were the binding and building ancestors of this place' (*CM*, p. 145). Kingston continually suggests that the Chinese American role in the metamorphosis of America accords the China men a right of ownership of the land, predominantly through her creation of atavistic narratives. Ancestry, and the evocation of ancestral connection, is one way in which a sense of belonging is asserted.[38] Here, Kingston constantly evokes the language of ancestry in order to press her – and her male forbears' – claims to American territory. Repeated references to ancestorship include the very chapter titles: 'Grandfather of the Sierra Nevada Mountains', 'The American Father', 'The Great-Grandfather of the Sandalwood Mountains', all of which signify ownership. In another case, a sense of ownership is asserted forcefully through the actions of the railroad grandfather Ah Goong. In a memorable scene, this grandfather of the railroad urinates off a mountain face and then masturbates: '"I am fucking the world", he said. The world's vagina was big ... he fucked the world' (*CM*, p. 132). Ah Goong literally marks his territory; and his act of masturbation is both an attempt to master his environment in a rape-like act, and to lay claim to his territory, so that the act of masturbation becomes a kind of sexual graffiti. It is a literalised image of the interpenetration between a human and his environment that Kolodny describes above. In this example, Kingston links the language of procreation with possession to intervene in dominant cultural narratives of origins in an ironic parody of the creation myth. The sexual defilement of the landscape in this manner also has ironic resonances for notions of national (read racial) purity in the context of the assumed link between nationality and territoriality. In her work on metaphors of experience and history of the frontier, Kolodny charts the growth of frontier metaphors of 'psychosexual dramas of men intent on possessing a virgin continent';[39] and the ways in which this 'land – as woman symbolisation'[40] engendered an 'eroticised intimacy with the environment'.[41] As Kingston took up myths of colonisation like the *Robinson Crusoe*/Lo Bun Sun story and undermined them, here she engages with these metaphors and fantasies of sexual control over the land. By depicting her characters' re-enactment of the 'psychosexual drama', Kingston appropriates this metaphor for *her* pioneers' experience, while at the same time firmly locating the Asian American creation and experience of the frontier within a dominant psychohistory of the frontier.

The gendered landscape and the emasculated China man

Kingston's appropriation of dominant metaphors of the frontier is also gendered. Kolodny demonstrates how the metaphor and experience of the frontier have always been different for men and for women. While men, as I discuss above, reacted to the frontier in sexual terms, with images and acts of sexual domination, women responded with Edenic metaphors and images and acts of tending the land. Rather than producing the urge to dominate, encounters with the frontier for women produced the desire to domesticate, as Kolodny writes, to 'domesticate the strangeness of America'.[42] This metaphor is also used by Kingston in relation to her China men. At the very beginning of the text, Kingston indicates that she intends to present the China men's experience in America as not only an experience of estrangement, but also of emasculation, through her retelling of the story 'On Discovery'.[43] The thesis that the immigrant experience is emasculating is continued when Kingston depicts the Chinese American immigrants responding to the land in female terms by tending a garden:

> For recreation, because he was a farmer and as an antidote for the sameness of the cane, he planted a garden near the huts ... he ticked off in a chant the cuttings, seeds and bulbs he had brought across the ocean – pomelo, kumquat, which is 'golden luck', tangerines, citron also known as five fingers and Buddha's hand, ginger, bitter melon and other kinds of melon. (*CM*, p. 106)

For Bak Goong, the act of tending the land is a literal domestication: the transformation of the land into a more Asian landscape through the flora. Tending a garden thus is a strategy to combat the estrangement accompanying immigration. Kingston also shows how the processes of immigration have been emasculating by locating Bak Goong's reaction to the landscape within a female tradition of *gardening* as well as *conquering* the frontier, since the China men's response to the frontier is also allied with the male desire for domination that Kolodny discusses. As Ah Goong sought to engage in intercourse with the land, so Bak Goong and the other sugarcane workers worked the land in sexual terms:

> The land was ready to be sown. They bagged the slips in squares of cloth tied over their shoulders. Flinging the seed cane into ditches, Bak Goong wanted to sing like a farmer in an opera. When his bag was empty, he stepped into the furrow and turned the seed cane so the nodes were to the sides, nodes on either side of the stick like an animal's eyes. He filled the trenches and patted the pregnant earth. (*CM*, p. 105)

Here, echoing Ah Goong's masturbation, Bak Goong impregnates the land and through this becomes a literal progenitor of the American landscape. Through these images of insemination, Kingston both echoes a long dominant cultural tradition of responses to the frontier and also once again asserts a paternity claim to the land on behalf of her China men forbears, underscoring her assertion that living in – and changing – the environment ought to entitle ownership. Kolodny writes that the role the Asian American presence had in the American West was in transforming the agrarian landscape into an 'industrial frontier,'[44] which is illustrated here in the stories of Ah Goong, Bak Goong and Bak Sook Goong, as instances of the physical terrain and cultural landscape changing as a result of the initial cultural contact between Chinese and Americans. The physical terrain in one case is actually named after those who trans-formed it: Mokoli'i Island in Hawai'i is known as 'Chinaman's Hat', so language, in the form of nomenclature, is used as a way of further inscribing the claim to territory. Kingston writes that: 'It's a tribute to the pioneers to have a living island named after their workhat' (*CM*, p. 91). Through these images, Kingston seems to suggest that it is the transformation of the land that makes Chinese into Chinese Americans. It is also significant that the 'railroad demons' set up a contest between different ethnic groups in building the railroad, which can be symbolically read as a contest for colonisation: 'Day shifts raced against night shifts, China Men against Welshmen, China men against Irishmen, China Men against Injuns and black demons' (*CM*, p. 138). In this quotation, 'Americans' are simply not present in the contest for ownership of the land; rather, new immigrant groups are seen engaged in competition for possession of the land, and, through that, for national belonging.

However, Kingston ultimately questions whether changing the land and inhabiting the land can lead to a claim to territory. Like Kolodny, Kingston recognises that within an American legal discursive system ownership must be circumscribed textu-ally in the form of legal or historical documentation in order to be legitimate. Textual possession both facilitates and engenders physical possession. It is a prerequisite, although the validity of such a requirement is also queried by Kingston.

Claiming America

In *China Men*, therefore, we see Kingston, via the stories of her China men forbears, interrogating the ways in which 'American-ness', as a sign of 'national' belonging, is engendered and inscribed. This takes place on the various battlefields of identity: language, cultural practices and occupations.[45] Ah Goong mistakenly believes that his part in the creation of the new frontier will make him American: 'Only Americans could have done it … he was an American for having built the railroad' (*CM*, p. 144). Some of the other China men believe that American dress, names and pastimes will create their Americanness: they name themselves Ed, Woodrow, Roosevelt and Worldster, go to tea parties and 'looked all the same Americans' in suits (*CM*, p. 65).[46]

The need for Americanness to be inscribed officially as nationality and citizenship becomes increasingly clear to the China men, who are barred from citizenship because of their ethnicity. As 'The Laws' section tells us, 'national origin' upon which the qualification for citizenship is based, did not mean 'country of birth' until 1965, and so Asian Americans were barred from naturalising for many more years. In the China men who yearn to be fully fledged citizens, the confidence men who pose as 'citizenship judges' find easy prey: 'The demon said "I Citizenship judge invite you to be US citizen. Only one bag gold." Ah Goong was thrilled. What an honour' (*CM*, p. 141). The citizenship judges prey on the need for official recognition of Americanness; as one China man notes: 'he was already a part of this new country, but now he had it in writing' (*CM*, p. 141). Of course, Kingston's intention here is ironic: the official circumscription of citizenship that Ah Goong has acquired is worthless. His misplaced faith in the authority of official texts is emphasised: 'If he got kidnapped, Ah Goong planned, he would whip out his Citizenship paper and show that he was an American' (*CM*, p. 147). The precarious nature of 'official' 'legal' documentation is illustrated further when the Hall of Records burns down:

> Citizenship papers burned, Residency certificates, passenger
> lists, Marriage certificates – every paper a China man
> wanted for citizenship and legality burned in that fire. An
> authentic citizen, then, had no more papers than an alien
> … every Chinaman was reborn out of that fire a citizen.
> (*CM*, p. 149)

Significantly, the citizenship judges/confidence men take
advantage of the China men at the point at which the labour on
the railroad ceases because of a battle over wages, the moment
when the China men feel most insecure in their new country. In
a final act of injustice, once the railroad is finished, the China
men are driven out, so the legitimation and recognition for
which they had toiled by working on the railroad are lost, and it
is tellingly at this point that Ah Goong considers returning to
China.

Citizenship is also defined through contestation. As Mad
Sao 'proves' his Americanness by fighting in World War Two,
so Kingston tells us: 'Chinese Americans talk about how when
they set foot in China, they realise their Americanness' (*CM*, p.
287). The 'Vietnam Brother' who is given Q clearance (high-
level security clearance) also becomes aware of his Americanness: 'the government was certifying that the family was really
American, not precariously American but super-American'
(*CM*, p. 291); yet he is forced to choose between contesting
national allegiances, and it is by making his choice, for America,
that he receives Q clearance. Kingston ironically notes: 'maybe
that Grandfather's Citizenship judge was real and legal after all'
(*CM*, p. 291). Ultimately, though, this Vietnam brother rejects
his American allegiance as he realises that he remains loyal to
his Chinese identity too.[47] Uncle Bun comes to the same recognition, which is implied through his fear of the House Un-
American Activities Committee. Here, 'citizenship' or 'subjecthood', meaning 'under the authority or law of a country' or 'in
political and legal subjection to a country', whereby that country
must reciprocate with obligations to the individual, collapses,
becoming 'subject to', that is, conditional and provisional, and
also 'in subjection to', suggesting subordination and domination.

Ultimately, neither the Vietnam brother nor Uncle Bun can meet the demands that the dominant culture places upon them as citizens. By placing Chinese and American allegiances in contestation with each other, Kingston effectively exposes the ironies and pressures of the qualifications for citizenship and subjecthood in a country slow to reciprocate with legitimating, if not welcoming, gestures, as illustrated in 'The Laws' section of the text. Near the end of *China Men*, these conflicting national allegiances are represented symbolically in the Confucius[48] Hall: 'Sun Yat Sen's and Chiang Kai Shek's pictures were on the stage next to the American and Chinese flags' (*CM*, p. 261).

The ironies of citizenship are also echoed in Kingston's father's experience at the Immigration station on Angel Island. The president of the 'Self Governing Organisation' invites Kingston's father to join, which will entitle him to vote and protect his immigration interests. The ironies of statesmanship are exposed when the president tells Kingston's father that he 'won his office by having been on the island the longest' (*CM*, p. 55), which echoes the Lo Bun Sun story and highlights the ironies of Anglo colonisation. Furthermore, the association itself is seen in an ironic light, since none of the newly arrived men possess any of the benefits of democratic citizenship; as detainees they are neither free nor franchised, and the 'Self Governing Organisation' does not seem to contribute to the advancement of citizenship for its members. The creation of a micro nation state on Angel Island also underscores the China men's desire for American citizenship and their desperate need for a sense of official 'belonging'. Significantly, the tale of the China man's experience on Angel Island, his long detention and repeated interrogation, is revealed to be the story of the 'legal' father. Thus, the ironies of the legal process are exposed when juxtaposed with the altogether more congenial narrative of the illegal immigrant father, who is made welcome: 'Chinatown seemed to be waiting to welcome him' (*CM*, p. 54). Significantly at this juncture, the heightened sensation of the American land beneath his feet serves to engender in him the feeling of belonging. *Terra incognita* becomes *terra firma*: 'He disciplined his legs to step confidently, as if they belonged where they walked. He felt the concrete through his shoes' (*CM*, p. 54). Here, as earlier, physical contact with the ground is seen to constitute a sense of belonging. The earlier cries of the new immigrants to 'let me land' (*CM*, p. 58) take on new significance. Once more, physical contact with the terrain psychologically confirms territoriality. This is in opposition to cartographical documentation, which, as a means of inscribing territory, is, like historical and legal inscriptions, questioned by Kingston in *China Men*. Benedict Anderson asserts that maps are an instrument of power like legal or historical texts, because as self-protective and self-legitimating devices, they are used by the state to imagine its domain.[49] As 'a form of totalising classification',[50] maps are treated with equal mistrust, and in *China Men* cartographic inscriptions of the world and of reality are highlighted as subjective as well as unreliable:

> The villagers unfolded their maps of the known world, which differed: turtles and elephants supported the continents, which were islands on their backs; in other cartographies, the continents were mountains with China the middle mountain, Han Mountain or Tang Mountain or the Wah Republic, a Gold Mountain to its west on some maps and to the east on others. (*CM*, p. 49)

What is 'known' is shown to be precarious and shifting, so that through cartographic uncertainty Kingston further questions epistemological certainty, here of the cartographic text. Subjective cartographies do not coincide with supposedly more referential maps: Gold Mountain – the mythologised site of Chinese dreams of America – cannot be fixed geographically, as Kingston shows; the Gold Mountain yearned for by the China man 'coming to claim the Gold Mountain, his own country' (*CM*, p. 54), is not where it is expected to be. Kingston tells us that one of the China men went to 'live in California, which *some say* is the real Gold Mountain anyway' (*CM*, p. 75; emphasis mine). Thus, real and imagined cartographies co-exist alongside real and imagined sites, again rendering problematic assumptions about the referentiality of cartographic texts. It is, therefore, worth noting that the trajectories created and through them the territories claimed by Kingston for her China men ancestors, are the work of someone with 'no map sense' (*CM*, p. 198).

The *Li Sao*: ex-centricity reinscribed

The *Li Sao* epic elegy, retold by Kingston towards the end of *China Men*, both echoes and draws together the China men's stories. Ch'u Yuan, 'wronged and exiled' (*CM*, p. 251), was forced to leave his kingdom and wander for the rest of his life in barbarian lands, where he finally died by drowning. Kingston always intends her retelling of myths to comment on the narrative, and here she uses the *Li Sao* to emphasise how displacement leads to state- and law-sanctioned dispossession. We are told: 'he had to leave the Centre; he roamed in the outer world for the rest of his life, twenty years' (*CM*, p. 250). The story of Ch'u Yuan, like the China men's stories, is the story of the 'ex-centric'. The 'ex-centric', in Linda Hutcheon's definition, is someone who finds themselves at the margins, and 'ex-centricity' is the state of being at the margin, the border or the edge. The ex-centric is marginal in terms of race, gender, ethnicity, class, sexuality or social role, as defined in opposition to a centre. Once again, definition takes place through contestation and here the challenge to the centre comes from the border. Thus here too the process of definition, as in Kolodny's model of frontier evolution, is an oppositional paradigm. Hutcheon writes that 'the ex-centric relies on the centre for its definition',[51] as in Kolodny's model where the frontier was the result of the confrontation between two interest groups. Kingston's China men are all ex-centrics. In Hutcheon's words, the ex-centric is 'the off-center, ineluctably identified with the center it desires but is denied'.[52] The constant yearning for citizenship by the ex-centric China men marks their desire for centricity.

The China men's ex-centricity results from their diasporic move from China as centric citizens to America where they are in exile. Centricity is defined by context. The China men become ex-centric in the context of the American nation state, where they find themselves non-members and are therefore relegated to the cultural, legal and social margins. *China Men* constitutes a potent challenge to ethnocentrism, as the previously silent, displaced China men's history and validity are reasserted by Kingston. She writes of the China men: 'You say with the few words and the silences: No stories. No past. No China' (*CM*, p. 18). The inscription of Chinese American history and, through this, the shattering of the ex-centric's silence, results in a contestation of (but not for) the centre and its historical legitimising texts. The project of claiming America for her ex-centric ancestors involves Kingston in a reordering of culture by revaluing personal and subjective histories in opposition to monolithic history, so the 'official' text of history inscribed in 'The Laws' section co-exists with the vernacular histories of the China men grand/fathers.[53] The homogenising tendency of frontier literary history described by Kolodny as the 'grand narrative of discovery and progress' is revised in the face of heterogenising testimonies like those of the China men, with the accompanying attentiveness of the text to the subjectivity of the enunciating presence. However, this does not result in a move on the part of the ex-centric from the margin to the centre, although this desire is displayed by Kingston's father, who 'inked each piece of our own laundry with the word *Centre*' (*CM*, p. 18). As Hutcheon observes: 'it does not invert the valuing of centers into that of peripheries and borders'.[54] Kingston recognises that her father cannot tell her 'how we landed in a country where we are eccentric people' (*CM*, p. 18). Rather, the *presence* of the ex-centric, and the articulation of the ex-centric's perspective, story and history, contests the epistemological status and homogenising tendency of the dominant cultural and physical centre, which is America, and the Anglo American perspective. Thus, dominant versions of history are revealed to be erroneous, and America is located geographically both to the east and the west of China, depending on which text one consults. The presence of the ex-centric's perspective engenders the recognition that historical, auto/biographical and cartographic as well as fictional representations are never value-neutral. The new significance of the ex-centric or marginal perspective accompanies a recognition of the value of heterogeneity, so that otherness emerges in a positive light, while remaining defined in opposition to the centre, as Kingston recognises:

> our dog tags had *O* for religion and *O* for race because neither black nor white ... some kids said *O* was for 'Oriental', but I knew it was for 'Other' because the Filipinos, the Gypsies, and the Hawaiian boy were *O*s. (*CM*, pp. 269–270)

By re-interpreting the frontier as 'a specifiable first moment on that liminal borderland between distinct cultures', Kolodny suggests that a previously 'narrow Eurocentric design' is decentred. Thus, Kolodny's vision of a new literary frontier history coincides with the project of challenging centres and revaluing borders. Texts and peoples previously liminal due to their ethnicity, race or gender become the centre of attention, because, as Kolodny notes, 'the frontier is displaced always to the geographical edges'. Thus, the edge – geographical, cultural and literary – destabilises the centre as the emphasis shifts. The emphasis on frontier literary history texts like Maxine Hong Kingston's *China Men* ultimately forces an opening up of the question of literariness. By way of its multi-media texture, *China Men* forces a questioning of what constitutes not just a literary, but also an historical or auto/biographical text. *China Men* thus demonstrates that it is not just the centre which does not hold, but neither do those boundaries between different genres and discourses, so that the official voice of history co-exists alongside the more marginal diasporic voices of the ex-centric China men.

Tripmaster Monkey: His Fake Book
(1989)

> I wanted to sing the Chinese American self. (Maxine Hong
> Kingston, 'Talking with the Woman Warrior' (1989))

> In the novel which I'm working on now, *Tripmaster
> Monkey: His Fake Book*, my 23-year-old protagonist,
> Wittman Ah Sing, works to bring theater back to life. He
> imagines its beginnings in mythic China, but all the while
> alarmed that his roots are too exotic and non-American. I
> mean for Wittman to have a slangy, hip style. I hope that
> you hear a voice that is very different from the ones I've
> used before. (Maxine Hong Kingston, 'Singing Madly in
> the Valley', from *Through the Black Curtain* (1987))

After the critical clamour that followed the publication of
Kingston's first two books, the quiet bemusement of critics
which was the predominant response to *Tripmaster Monkey:
His Fake Book* came as quite a change. To be sure, many of the
earliest reviews of the book were reacting to the aggressive
marketing of 'her first novel' by Kingston's publishers. Critics
also reacted badly to the frenetic pace and insistent – perhaps
also incessant – narrative monologue of the central character,
Wittman Ah Sing. A brief survey of some of the responses finds
a mixed bag of comments: in a review entitled 'Manic Monologue' Anne Tyler found the novel 'exhausting';[1] Caroline Ong
declared it 'at times bordering on the incomprehensible';[2]
Pamela Longfellow went further, declaring it 'awful';[3] Kingston's
future Berkeley colleague Gerald Vizenor criticised Kingston's

over-reliance upon coincidence;[4] and Nicci Gerrard summed the book up as 'bitter repetitious paranoia'.[5] Not all of the reviews were negative though; writing in *The Nation*, John Leonard described Kingston's 'Novel of the Sixties' as 'an encyclopedic postmodern narrative that references, embraces, and absorbs a dizzying variety of sources from all cultures and eras';[6] and fellow writer Bharati Mukherjee praised the text's 'remarkable display of wit and rage' (despite also finding the novel somewhat 'bloated').[7] In evaluating these responses, E.D. Huntley muses that the aspects of Kingston's novel that flummoxed readers were

> Wittman's disorganized, unpunctuated, uneven, unstoppable free ranging monologues ... an unheroic protagonist, a disjointed rambling narrative of episodic adventures, and a fractured chronology ... the vast sprawling plot ... ending ...with ... a manic free-ranging monologue about life, war, peace, racism, heritage, culture, and the American identity.[8]

Readers familiar with postmodern fiction will find this description of the characteristics of Kingston's novel typical of the form, since formal features of postmodern fiction such as linguistic word play, free-form plot, self-reflexivity, narrative framing techniques (images of stories-within-stories abound in the novel), exhaustive intertextual references, a paranoid and sceptical perspective, the commodification of the past and of cultural artefacts, parody and pastiche (the subtitle is 'his fake book'), are all to be found in abundance in *Tripmaster Monkey*. Indeed, departing somewhat from more usual comparisons of Kingston's writing with other forms of ethnic literature, *Tripmaster* invites comparison with such landmark postmodern fictions as William Burroughs' *The Naked Lunch* or Bret Easton Ellis' *Less Than Zero*. What especially marks out Kingston's novel, though, is the sophisticated braiding of these quintessentially postmodernist techniques with a form of ethnic self-empowerment evident in Wittman's agency and action. Viewed in this way, Kingston's novel emerges as a fiction of 'insurgency', in the manner suggested by Robert Siegle in his influential work *Surburban Ambush: Downtown Writing and the Fiction of Insurgency* (1989), in which he identified a form of creative output – 'guerrilla action' – which actively seeks to destabilise and undermine privileged perspectives, replacing them with something which, if nothing else, promotes the cultural stance and politics of marginalised groups.[9] As Kingston put it in an interview at the time of *Tripmaster*'s publication: 'The artist comes in and breaks up the facts, breaks up the stereotypes, breaks up the static way that most of us look at the world'.[10]

Published in 1989, *Tripmaster Monkey: His Fake Book* is nevertheless undoubtedly a novel of and about the 1960s. In a 1989 interview with William Satake Blauvelt, Kingston said that 'I wanted to write the story of the 60s' (p. 80), and confessed that

> The 1960s were some of the most important years of my life and they go into forming me and the country the way it is now. I wanted to write a story about that period that came after the beatniks and before the hippies.[11]

Tripmaster Monkey actually only covers a two-month period in 1963 in the life of young would-be beatnik, Chinese American graduate Wittman Ah Sing, but through a series of nine relatively unconnected episodes, Kingston manages to capture the mood and tone of the whole era, as well as providing a keyhole portrait of life for Wittman in the Berkeley–Bay Area locale. This is quite deliberate: the epigraph to the text reads: 'This fiction is set in the 1960s, a time when some events appeared to occur months or even years anachronistically'. As many commentators have observed, the novel also conforms to many of the stylistic traits of the picaresque genre of fiction, in which the narrative tracks the escapades of an individual, often rogue-like character through an episodic structure. The nine episodes or chapters which comprise *Tripmaster Monkey* track Wittman's literal journey through Berkeley and its environs, and his metaphorical journey in search of his identity. Along the way, he encounters a series of characters, including would-be sexual partners, his future wife Taña, soul-mates, friends and relatives, all of whom ultimately all come together to help Wittman stage a play at the culmination of the novel.

The opening episode, 'Trippers and Askers' introduces Wittman, who is wandering around a foggy San Francisco and pondering his existence as a young Chinese American graduate. From the outset, Kingston establishes the importance of the environment of Berkeley in the novel;[12] the opening lines read:

> Maybe it comes from living in San Francisco, city of clammy humors and foghorns that warn and warn – omen, o-o-men, o dolorous omen, o dolors of omens – and not enough sun[13]

as well as Wittman's fondness for linguistic puns and his predilection for a hip, slang-style of speech. As the epigraphal comment by Kingston suggested at the opening of this chapter, Wittman's language captures the style and tone of Berkeley hip-cool, and his travels locate him firmly in the countercultural, alternative landscape of Berkeley in the 1960s. Kingston's imaginative evocation of images of the sixties is distinct. Wittman's existence is thus firmly located in a 'countercultural continuum' – sandwiched between the Beat generation of the 1950s and the hippies of the 1970s. Utilising the specific lexicon of the 60s though, the title of this section, 'Trippers and Askers', also pays homage to the drug culture prevalent in Berkeley, as elsewhere, at this time, since 'trippers' were drug-takers, and this is a theme which resurfaces later in the novel too. Wittman travels to meet a fellow graduate, a young Chinese American would-be actress, Nanci Lee, with whom he has coffee during which they chat about life, ancestry, identity and belonging – both literal and figurative, as well as the possibilities for life after college: 'Is there life after Berkeley?' he asks her (*TM*, p. 17). This encounter provides a stage for Wittman's first treatise on his identity and his life – the first of many that pepper the novel. In many ways, each episode, each encounter with a new character, is merely a fictional device to give Wittman someone to whom to talk. For talking is what Wittman does best, and does relentlessly, throughout this episode and others, so much so that it is hard for other characters to get a word in at all.[14] In this sense, 'Trippers and Askers' is one very long trip: Wittman's inward trip into his imagination.

'Trippers and Askers' is also a reference to another celebrated literary trip: Walt Whitman's 'Song of Myself' from his collection *Leaves of Grass* (1855), which is a notable inter-text to *Tripmaster Monkey*. 'Trippers and Askers' is in fact a direct quotation from 'Song of Myself', as is 'Linguists and Contenders' and 'A Song for Occupations', the titles of two of the episodes that follow. Clearly, Wittman's name is also a reference to Walt Whitman himself, and the two texts have much in common. Like *Tripmaster Monkey*, 'Song of Myself' is an extended confessional drama of and meditation upon identity, democracy and belonging in America, gender, race and embodiment. Just as Whitman, in the mid-nineteenth century, sought to locate his 'democratic vistas', so Kingston's Wittman seeks to do the same in the mid-twentieth century. Much has been written of the 'Beat' writers Allen Ginsberg, Jack Kerouac and others (all, incidentally, also explicitly evoked in *Tripmaster Monkey*) as the natural inheritors of Walt Whitman's literary mode; so too could be said of Maxine Hong Kingston, in this book at least. Kingston herself noted in 1990:

> in writing *Tripmaster Monkey* – I just lifted lines from *Leaves of Grass*. You would think they were modern Sixties' slang – 'Trippers and Askers' and 'Linguists and Contenders Surround Me' – all of that – 'Song of the Open Road,' 'Song of Occupations' – I just took those for title headings for my book.[15]

Episode two, 'Linguists and Contenders', opens with Wittman writing rather than speaking for a change. He is working on his play, a complex and involved endeavour: 'After two thousand days of quest, which takes a hundred chapters to tell, and twenty-four acts, seven days to perform' (*TM*, p. 42). He leaves work upon his play to travel to labour of a different kind, at a department store, where Wittman is employed as a salesman in the Toy Department. This provides a platform for Wittman to rail against consumerism and the commodification of cultural life, a recurrent theme in the novel:

> When he was a kid, he thought he could be happy forever
> working in a store. ... Is this malcontentedness what
> comes with a liberal arts education? The way they taught
> you to think at school was to keep asking what's really
> going on. What's that thing at the end of this assembly
> line *for*? Why merchandising? Why business? Why
> money? Who are these stockholders? What else have they
> got their fingers into? Are any of the holdings in bomb
> commodities? (*TM*, p. 45)

Disillusioned with this commercial world, Wittman first tries to
make the store's policies more ethical:

> 'I move that we operate on a profit-sharing plan.' 'Let's
> run this store on co-op principles.' 'I move that we reserve
> one table in the Garden Lanai for feeding the poor.' 'Does
> selling candy to children contribute to their good?' 'I move
> that the Sports Department stop selling guns and ammo.'
> (*TM*, p. 61)

yet when this fails, he resorts to subverting the relentless sales
ethic of the store by staging a sexual encounter between a
'Barbie Bride' and a monkey toy for young children shopping
with their mothers at the store, thus rejecting this existence and
all it symbolises. Not surprisingly, Wittman's actions end his
employment at the store: 'Wittman walked' (*TM*, p. 65). Later in
the novel, Wittman knowingly observes that 'In this society,
retailers define saneness. If you hate the marketplace, and can't
sell, and don't buy much, you're crazy' (*TM*, p. 237).

Wittman's trip

The novel is heavily steeped in the ideology of the sixties'
counterculture: the drug experimentation which started with
the Beats and Harvard psychologist Timothy Leary, and which
represented the rejection of dominant and repressive social
values; the search for a higher creative consciousness through
psychedelic states; the communal 'trip festivals'; the sit-ins, the
love-ins, the tune-ins, turn-ons and drop-outs, which define the

life of Wittman and his friends. The following two sections of the novel, 'Twisters and Shouters' and 'The Winners of the Party', work as a diptych showcasing Wittman's trip into his imagination, when he first recites from his play-to-be, and where he develops his relationship with his future wife, Taña. Newly unemployed, he travels to a party in Oakland, where he is described by a fellow partygoer as 'the Chinese Beatnik' (*TM*, p. 82). At the party, Kingston stages a Burroughs-like drug trip where the partygoers describe their hallucinations, in an extended passage that stretches for nearly three pages without a break. The scene, as a collective imaginary experience, also prefigures the imaginative community Wittman will create later through his staged play. Here, Wittman is asked to be one of the trippers' guides – the 'tripmaster': 'Excuse me, but some of us have dropped L.S.D. Will you be our guide? We should have gotten a guide ahead of time. You wouldn't mind, would you' one asks (*TM*, p. 102). Kingston explains that 'Those were the days when heads prepared their trips carefully, and chose a watchman who promises to remain straight. Just in case. At sea, a shore' (*TM*, p. 102).[16] Wittman's role as tripmaster here is pivotal: hereafter he becomes the reader's own master as he guides the way through life, art, philosophy and love in the rest of the novel, on his own inward trip. Wittman's trip is also an expression of the intertwined strands of his cultural and political dissent, what sixties' countercultural magazine *Fuck You* paradigmatically described as 'pacifism, unilateral disarmament ... non-violent resistance ... multilateral indiscriminate aperture conjugation, anarchy, world federalism ... the LSD communarium ... and group-gropes'. By way of this vision, Wittman invites the reader to become a tripper too; and to partake of the experience he is able to offer as an artist. At the party, Wittman also meets Taña, who will become his partner, and later his wife. He immediately knows that he has found a soulmate: 'She's melting my loneliness' he says (*TM*, p. 113).

Monkey King: *Journey to the West*

> 'MONKEY' is the spirit of the protagonist, Witman Ah
> Sing, who is a showman and a trickster. (Maxine Hong
> Kingston, 'Plans')

> I am really: the present-day U.S.A. incarnation of the King
> of the Monkeys. (Wittman Ah Sing, *Tripmaster Monkey*)

Wittman's trip ends when he describes to 'the winners of the
party' – the party hosts, Lance and Sunny, Nanci and Taña – the
plot of his newly envisioned play. Loosely based upon the
Chinese classic, *Journey to the West*, the play also includes
elements from two other traditional Chinese sources, *The
Romance of the Three Kingdoms* and *The Water Margin*, and
these texts comprise three of the most famous Chinese classical
works of literature. The framing narrative of *Journey to the
West* provides both the skeletal outline of Wittman's play and a
useful metaphor for the figure of Wittman himself. Wu Cheng-
en's sixteenth-century novel *Hsi Yu Chi/Journey to the West*
features an unusual hero, 'Monkey Sun', a monkey figure
hatched from a stone egg and gifted with magical powers by a
Taoist master. Monkey is chosen to accompany the Buddhist
monk Tripitaka (T'ang San-tsang – a real historical figure) on
his journey to India, where he will be given sacred texts to take
back to China. Monkey jumps through a waterfall into the
Kingdom of the Monkeys and this transforms him into the
Monkey King. Henceforth a semi-supernatural figure, Monkey
is capable of defending Tripitaka against a range of perils that
they encounter, including the 'White Bone Demon', as well as
more mortal enemies. His ability to metamorphose into seventy-
two transformations from animals to the inanimate, his skill at
defending himself with a magic pole that can enlarge or shrink,
his invisibility when necessary and the magic power that enables
him to somersault long distances make him a formidable figure.
His prowess is described by Yan Gao:

> In battles against monsters, his special trick is his ability to
> assume seventy-two forms, metamorphosing into plants
> (melons and peaches), flying beasts (phoenixes, crows,

eagles, sparrows, bats, and woodpeckers), quadrupeds (rats, hares, tigers, elephants, badgers, and pangolins), aquatic animals (shrimps, crabs, fish and snakes), insects (mosquitoes, flies, moths, fleas, bees, butterflies, ants, dragonflies, worms, and light bugs), buildings (temples), deities and monsters (God Er-lang, the Great Immortal of Naked Feet, and the Bull Monster-King), and even human beings (monks, children, young ladies, elderly ladies, and old men). Every one of the eighty-four thousand hairs on his body can change into whatever shape or substance he desires. With his magic power he can make a somersault over one hundred and eight thousand *li*, make himself invisible, travel freely to heaven and hell, and follow the sun and the moon. Metal cannot break him, water cannot drown him, and fire cannot burn him.[17]

Monkey's significance as a Chinese culture figure should likewise not be underestimated. In his study of classic Chinese literature, C. T. Hsia writes of this text, as well as *The Romance of the Three Kingdoms* and *The Water Margin*, that 'to this day they remain the most beloved novels among the Chinese', and of the figure of Monkey he observes that

> The character of Monkey as finally shaped by Wu Ch'eng-en also suggests such mythical heroes as Prometheus and Faust in his defiance of established authority and quest for knowledge and power.[18]

Similarly, Yan Gao observes that 'the Monkey King is a beloved character to the Chinese, a symbol of courage, wisdom, resourcefulness and humor'.[19] It is less these features that Kingston appropriates, though, than Monkey's artfulness as a trickster figure.[20] Kingston's use of the Monkey King in her portrait of Wittman Ah Sing is itself artful. As Diane Simmons notes, Kingston makes Wittman become 'a new Monkey King by systematically interweaving into American culture a Monkey image'.[21] Wittman, like Monkey, is an in-between figure. Just as Monkey inhabits the space between mortality and immortality, so Wittman moves between two cultures, 'between worlds' to use Amy Ling's memorable phrase.[22] Kingston also draws upon

Journey to the West's game-like structure and many game metaphors in her depiction of the playful yet cynical, rebel-like, countercultural figure of Wittman, who dodges his way through life. In 1989 she stated her intention thus: 'As I wrote about the '60s, I began to understand that the spirit of the monkey has come to America. You see in the Buddhist story he goes to India, but I have him continuing on and he arrives in America in the 1960s.'[23]

If Monkey serves as Tripitaka's guide, and Wittman as the trippers' guide, then Kingston arrogates herself the role of Wittman's guide. In *Journey to the West*, the goddess figure of Kwan (sometimes Kuan) Yin, the Goddess of Mercy, guides – and sometimes controls – Monkey. She tells him she 'is trying to keep you on the straight and narrow for your own good'.[24] Hsia defines her actions thus: 'she succors the pilgrims on numerous occasions' but nevertheless also seems to 'be at times patently cruel in tormenting them needlessly'.[25] Kingston describes her influence:

> I think of my narrator now as Kuan Yin (goddess of mercy). This is a big change – a narrator who people can see right away is a woman. She is always helping the women characters out in there, giving Wittman a bad time.[26]

Although Wittman's consciousness dominates the narrative perspective, Kingston/Kuan Yin interrupts frequently, often offering ironic commentary upon Wittman's actions, or offering advice. For instance, at the end of 'A Song for Occupations', we find this comment:

> There. Wittman Ah Sing had gotten married, found a venue for a theater, found his grandmother, who gave him money that he did not have to report. Good work. Phone the wife, and so to bed. A reader doesn't have to pay more money for the next chapter or admission to the show if there's going to be a show; you might as well travel on with our monkey for the next while. (*TM*, p. 268)

Kingston's technique of ironic interjection pays homage simultaneously to both Chinese and American literary traditions. It is common for classical Chinese texts to 'signpost' for the reader at the end of sections,[27] as Kingston does at the end of several of the episodes in *Tripmaster*; yet this is also a technique recognisable in much postmodern fiction. Famously, in John Fowles' *The French Lieutenant's Woman* (1969) we find this example:

> And so ends the story. What happened to Sarah, I do not know – whatever it was, she never troubled Charles again in person, however long she may have lingered in his memory. This is what most often happens. People sink out of sight, drown in the shadows of closer things.[28]

This can be compared with the closing lines of *Tripmaster Monkey*:

> And they *lost*. The clanging and banging fooled us, but now we know – they lost. Studying the mightiest war epic of all time, Wittman changed – beeen! – into a pacifist. Dear American monkey, don't be afraid. Here, let us tweak your ear, and kiss your other ear. (*TM*, p. 340)

In each case, the omniscient narrator 'interrupts' the story and thus creates 'a communicational bond between the teller and the told', as Linda Hutcheon puts it in her discussion of this technique in *The Politics of Postmodernism*.[29] This is a deliberate strategy on Kingston's part, as she asserts: 'I've achieved that omniscient narrator. Quite often, I say "you". I'm talking directly to the reader'.[30] Kingston's Monkey, like Monkey Sun in *Journey to the West*, is also a trickster.[31] In her study, *Writing Tricksters: Mythic Gambols in American Ethnic Literature*, Jeanne Rosier Smith describes *Tripmaster* as a 'full-blown trickster novel'.[32] She elaborates:

> Kingston ... not only ... employ[s] a trickster aesthetic formally but also introduce[s] a trickster protagonist as a model for personal and cultural identity. ... As both clown and savior, Wittman the Monkey trickster gathers a new American community to participate in his play, which wages a war against racism and celebrates the community as a place of healing.[33]

As Jeanne Rosier Smith, Gerald Vizenor and Henry Louis Gates, amongst others, have observed, the trickster is also a common figure in ethnic postmodernist writing. In what could serve as a description of Wittman's actions in the novel, William Hynes, for instance, writes: 'the logic of order and convergence, that is logos-centrism, or logocentrism, is challenged by another path, that random and divergent trail taken by that profane meta-player, the trickster'.[34]

The Water Margin and The Romance of the Three Kingdoms

In yet another postmodernist technique, Kingston couples her intertextual references to *Journey to the West* with a further, sometimes dizzying blend of literary sources, including two more classical Chinese texts, *The Water Margin* and *The Romance of the Three Kingdoms*. Like *Journey to the West*, both texts are of significance in Chinese culture and would be familiar to any Chinese reader. Both texts have also evolved over many years in Chinese culture, and befitting their appearance in Wittman's story, both too have evolved from oral versions. *The Romance of the Three Kingdoms*, especially, although usually designated a historical narrative, is described by Hsia as comprising 'compilations of oral material'.[35] *The Romance of the Three Kingdoms* has its origins in the third century AD, but became better-known as a novel in the fifteenth century (a further widely circulated version appeared in the seventeenth century). It relates many stories of battle and conquest, including the story of three brothers-in-arms, Liu Pei, Cho Cho and Sun Ch'uan, who vie for the throne of China, and the power struggle between the three kingdoms Shu, Wu and Wei, and their ensuing clashes, conquests and ultimately the deaths of the three brothers-in-arms. Kingston borrows freely from this source, selecting episodes and incidents at will which best represent Wittman's sensibility and mood at a particular moment. Possibly the most significant of these is the 'oath scene', which takes place in a peach orchard, and which Wittman incorporates into his play. Here, the three brothers-in-arms meet for the first time and swear allegiance to each other, and swear to die on the same day. In Wittman's version, each figure is played by his friends: Lance Kamiyama is Liu Pei, Wittman plays Gwan Goong (or Kuan Yu) and Charley plays Chang Fei. Foreshadowing her later novel, *The Fifth Book of Peace*, Kingston redraws the scene though, to emphasise peace rather than conflict. In Wittman's version, the scene stages a debate about how to oppose war itself. Representing the whole gamut of attitudes to war, each character speaks of war. Here is 'Chang Fei':

> My dove brother. My hawk brother. These peach trees are at their fullest and reddest bloom. We vow friendship. Repeat after me. 'We three – Liu Pei, Gwan Goong, and Chang Fei – though not born to the same families, swear to be brothers. Though born under different signs, we shall seek the same death day'. (*TM*, p. 144)

Wittman takes the role of the 'hawk' brother (pro-war); Lance the 'dove' brother (anti-war), although Wittman's character is eventually persuaded by the arguments of pacifism. This staged scene from the Chinese novel also introduces for the first time Wittman's on-going preoccupation with the question of how to craft theatrical representation without war, which becomes an increasingly important theme in the text; as Wittman declares 'I have to make a theater ... without a war' (*TM*, p. 190). Many of the literary representations upon which Wittman draws, including these three Chinese sources, depict or depend upon war for narrative progression. Wittman seeks to discard these elements of each narrative whilst retaining creative components of each story. Other episodes taken from *The Romance of the Three Kingdoms* appear throughout *Tripmaster Monkey* at later points as well, and like the oath scene are, to a greater or lesser extent, adapted by Wittman to become more pacifist, and community-affirming, in emphasis.

Like *The Romance of the Three Kingdoms*, *The Water Margin* by Shui-hu Chuan is also 'by and large recorded in a vernacular'.[36] Perhaps even more than the other Chinese texts utilised by Kingston, *The Water Margin* is an apposite text for

Wittman to adopt and adapt. C.T. Hsia writes that here 'we see the wholesale importation of oral conventions ... and in the absence of authentic history we see a conscious fabulation of pseudo-history ... several sagas of picaresque heroes depicted in settings of everyday truth ... its form remains synthetic'.[37] Although this is a description of *The Water Margin*, it could also describe Kingston's own book, with its references to 'conscious fabulation', 'pseudo-history' and the 'synthetic' form, all terms reminiscent of descriptions of postmodernist fiction. *The Water Margin* follows the escapades of a band of 108 outlaws who were active during the reign of Hui-tsung in the Northern Sung Dynasty (1101–25), before their surrender in 1121. A well-known and oft-told legend, C.T. Hsia observes that, like *The Romance of the Three Kingdoms*, Chinese authors 'frequently raided the legend' of *The Water Margin* for their own stories, as Kingston does here, so much so that it too constitutes 'a work of multiple authorship'.[38] *The Water Margin*, or *Outlaws of the Marsh* as it is also known, parallels Wittman's story as it depicts a group of marginal figures fighting against injustice and oppressive authority. Described by Diane Simmons as 'a kind of countercultural community', the outlaw characters eventually figure in Wittman's play in the section 'Bones and Jones', where they are rewritten as Chinese American pioneers and victims of racism in a strange mix of a Western and a history play.[39]

Ethnicity and resistance

As critics have noticed, the word 'trip' has many meanings in the novel and is used as both a noun and a verb.[40] The word also carries connotations of trickery, in the sense of 'tripping up' the reader. Certainly, the text's myriad literary and cultural allusions make for a challenging reading experience. In addition to the Chinese sources that I have already discussed at length, a brief tally finds references to: Tolstoy, Rilke, Whitman, Steinbeck, Kerouac, Twain, Stevenson, John Muir, John Fante, Carlos Bulosan, Gertrude Atherton, Jack London, Ambrose Bierce, Bret

Harte, Charlie Chaplin, J.D. Salinger, Shakespeare, Chin Yang
Lee, Marilyn Monroe, Emily Dickinson, Antonin Artaud, Dave
Brubeck, Louis Armstrong, John Cage, Spenser, Melville, George
Peppard, Mickey Rooney, James Dean, James Joyce, Walt Disney,
D.H. Lawrence, Henry Miller, Sheridan Le Fanu, Gertrude
Stein, Charles Olson, Lew Welch, T.S. Eliot, Thomas Hardy,
Anna May Wong, William Burroughs, Gary Snyder, Aaron
Copland, Debbie Reynolds, Samuel Pepys, Bruce Lee, Jade Snow
Wong, Katherine Hepburn, Myrna Loy, Anna Chennault,
Rudyard Kipling, Leroi Jones, Lorraine Hansberry, James
Baldwin, Lee Marvin, Steve McQueen, Gregory Peck, Robert
Mitchum, Clint Eastwood, Marlon Brando, Rita Hayworth,
John Wayne and Lin Yutang. Kingston has said that she wanted
the figure of Wittman to be 'made up of all that he knows, all
that he has read'.[41] Cultural acquisition in the novel becomes the
only currency of worth – 'Got no money. Got no home, got
story', Wittman says – in a novel once described as 'allusive' but
also 'elusive'.[42]

Just as simian imagery abounds in the text, so recurrent
motifs also include exclusion, combat and mobility, equally
features of *Journey to the West* as Wittman's own journey *in*
the West. Wittman's battle throughout the novel is against a
matrix of injustices, including war, racism, commercial exploita-
tion of the individual, state marginalisation of the individual,
and the erosion of civil liberties. How to fight oppression and
racism? is a question always on Wittman's mind.[43] Wittman's
solution is to create a theatre, which he sees as a means to estab-
lish the intimacy of community in an increasingly alienated
world – 'We need it' he says (*TM*, p. 141). He takes his inspiration for this from the cultural re/sources that he has repeatedly
evoked in the narrative. Kingston traces the evolution of Chinese
American theatre and the beginnings of Chinese American
immigration to the same moment:

> The pioneers built the West by putting on shows. The
> puppet theater in I street was the first theater in Sacra-
> mento. You can still see the arched entranceway to the
> Star Theater in Locke, the Chinese American town.

Marysville has a bun festival and parade to this day. In his Obie-award-winning play, 'The Dance and the Railroad,' David Henry Hwang, who is a violinist and son of a pianist, tells about two workers dancing during the strike on the Transcontinental Railroad. Of all the Chinese gods, the one who came with us to America, the one we brought with us, was Guan Goong, whose likeness used to appear in parades that went from the temple to the theater and from the theater to the temple.[44]

In a 1989 interview, Kingston wrote of her intention to show 'the history of theater from monkey theater and talk story theater';[45] and of Wittman's intention 'to create community by putting on theater'.[46] From the first rehearsal of his play in the section 'The Winners of the Party' onwards, the novel becomes increasingly bound up with Wittman's vision of a community-affirming theatrical event; 'we make theater, we make community' he says (TM, p. 261), echoing Kingston's own conviction that 'we are going to solve the world's problems with theater'.[47] The novel is replete with images of rejuvenation and salvation through art. Wittman's vision of the theatre is one of 'the life of the human soul receiving its birth through art' (TM, p. 276); a vision that is inextricably bound up with both his own history (his female relatives all worked in the theatre as 'Flora Dora' show girls),[48] and with Chinese American history, as he proudly states:

A company of one hundred great-great grandparents came over to San Francisco during the Gold Rush, and put on epic kung fu opera and horse shows. Soon the cities had six companies – not those six business companies – six theater companies – the Mandarin Theater, the last to die; the Great China Theater, which runs movies now. The difference between us and other pioneers, we did not come here for the gold streets. We came to play. And we'll play again. (TM, pp. 249–250)

Wittman's other theatrical influences include a range of sixties' radical playwrights, including the African American playwrights Leroi Jones, Lorraine Hansberry and James Baldwin. As Diane

Simmons notes, Kingston uses these figures to evoke a form of countercultural improvisional theatre, with which some of these playwrights were experimenting in the sixties and seventies, and in which vein Wittman casts his own production.[49]

Wittman's determination to create a community-affirming event is also a historically specific act that further evokes the ethos of sixties counterculture. The staging of a community event clearly echoes, for instance, the euphoric fervour that imbued the organisation of the Woodstock Festival held in August, 1969. As the many newspaper reports of the time observed, Woodstock became a community event that was to symbolise for a whole generation the possibilities of the counterculture. As the seminal counterculture historian Theodore Roszak put it in his influential 1969 book, *The Making of a Counterculture*, the efforts of disenchanted sixties' youth could 'discover new types of community, new family patterns, new sexual mores, new kinds of livelihood, new esthetic forms, new personal identities on the far side of power politics, the bourgeois home, and the consumer society', nothing if not a description of Wittman's endeavour.[50] Wittman's play also recalls Julian Beck's and Judith Malina's 1960s experimental theatrical enterprise, 'The Living Theatre', a hyper-self conscious theatre aware of its own artifice, in which actors announced their own roles, and in which the ending was left open, to allow for the possibility for audience participation (as does Wittman's play). As the French critic Pierre Biner described it, The Living Theatre would 'communicate the very taste of revolution'.[51]

Gradually Wittman's play comes together. He persuades the local Chinese Benevolent Association to host his play, and he enlists the help of his grandmother PoPo, his mother Ruby Long Legs and his aunties, his friends Nanci Lee, Lance and Sunny, his wife Taña and his friend from the department store, known in the novel as 'the Yale Younger Poet'. The following section, 'A Pear Garden in the West', sees Wittman stage a rehearsal of his play, which is a somewhat amorphous theatrical enterprise, part show and part revue, a manic fusion that incorporates snippets from many literary and cultural texts, compact versions of other plays; parodies of other show forms, such as the vaude-villian Siamese twin freak show that fills the section 'Bones and Jones'; spectacular show routines; and lengthy monologues on a variety of topics including Chinese American history and ethnic stereotyping; all of which culminates in an even more specta-cular firework display.

Wittman's fake book: 'a text of basic melodies'

> The years after the beatniks and before the hippies, our theater went dark. Wittman Ah Sing and his friends start a theater something like San Francisco's Asian American Theatre Company, New York's Pan Asian or L.A.'s East West Players. (Maxine Hong Kingston, 'The Little Dragon', from *Through the Black Curtain* (1987))

The literary trickster is often a parodic character. In her reading of the intertextual references in *Tripmaster*, A. Noelle Williams suggests that textual sources themselves – like *Journey to the West* – are parodied by Kingston, and so 'form a kind of collaboration in their mimetic relationship'.[52] Williams suggests that by way of this parody/mimesis, Kingston effectively connects her novel's preoccupations with a host of extra-textual references and meanings: 'The fake or copy no longer signifies faulty or unenlightened but reinvents itself as the real that only the enlightened can appreciate'.[53] Fakery, is of course, a doubly charged term in Kingston criticism, since it evokes the contro-versy surrounding Chinese American playwright Frank Chin's infamous excoriation in 1976 of Kingston's artistic technique as 'fake' and racist. Speculation has abounded that Kingston slyly based Wittman Ah Sing on the figure of Frank Chin, although this is something that Kingston has consistently publicly denied.[54] Nevertheless, the similarities are evident. In his extensive cor-respondence with Kingston in 1976, following the publication of *The Woman Warrior* (and when Kingston was starting to write *Tripmaster Monkey*), Frank Chin made repeated references to both the history of Chinese American theatre and to sources such as *The Romance of the Three Kingdoms*. The following, quite extensive quotation, is representative:

> Once there were three opera houses in Chinatown Frisco hot and heavy with hundred night five hours a night free for all versions of Kwan Kung's opera, THE ROMANCE OF THE THREE KINGDOMS. Kwan Kung was played by the strongest young man in Chinatown. The once upon a time Cantonese opera was soon a purely Chinaman expression as it adjusted language, and style, detail, event, and setting to changing world of the Chinamans at work on a new experience, making new language to define the new experience and made new history.
>
> In form, the opera is like the novel. The novel, ROMANCE OF THE THREE KINGDOMS is written to seem a collection of documents, various story teller's cheat sheets, doggerel and repeats of folk hearsay by different people writing at different times about the same historical event. … The novel makes James Joyce as simple as Dick an [sic] Jane of the Cantonese and the Chinamans.[55]

Chin's slang notwithstanding, a more accurate description of both Kingston's enterprise and Wittman's project is hard to imagine. Chin's correspondence with Kingston is written in slang, an often free-form, ra(n)ging style, which is also remarkably similar to Wittman's. Compare the following excerpts from Chin's letters with a passage from *Tripmaster*:

> I am not Chinese, just as my name is not Fido or Charlie Chan. I am a Chinaman. The China I come from hasn't been China for a Century and a half and exists only here, Chinese America.[56]
>
> I mean avant garde. What was new and socko in 1950, was Beat in Beatnik Frisco of the fifties. Lawrence Ferling-hetti's *City Lights Journal* of Spring 1955 was in the shadow of Alan Watts' giving up one form of Christianity for an Oriental religious philosophy he thought was better, Zen. What he found in Zen was the Christianity Kang Yu Wei has written into the old parlor game, in the late nineteenth century. … Once again, here I am, a

Chinaman who hates Charlie Chan the detective, sorting
out my clues.[57]

Bumkicked again. If King Kerouac, King of the Beats, were
walking here tonight, he'd see Wittman and think, 'Twinkling little Chinese.' Refute 'little.' Gainsay 'twinkling.' A
man does not twinkle. A man with balls is not little. As a
matter of fact, Kerouac didn't get 'Chinese' right either.
Bug football player white all-American jock Kerouac. Jock
Kerouac. I call into question your naming of me. I trust
your sight no more. You tell people by their jobs. And by
their race. And the wrong race at that. If Ah Sing were to
run into Kerouac – grab him by the lapels of his lumberjack
shirt. Pull him up on his toes. Listen here, you twinkling
little Canuck. What do you know, Kerouac? What do you
know? You don't know shit. I'm the American here. Fuck
Kerouac and his American road anyway. (*TM*, pp. 69–70)

These excerpts are representative of both Wittman's and Chin's
style. A lengthier perusal of Chin's epistolary outpourings to
Kingston (they are extensive) reveals that she has closely
captured Chin's trademark mix of invective, cultural nationalist
rant and flowing obscenity in the voice of Wittman (much is too
explicit and obscene to quote here). Deliberately intended or not,
it is clear that Kingston's novel is thus imbricated in the wider
history of the vexed debates about authenticity and ethnicity
that took place in the wake of the publication of *The Woman
Warrior*. Kingston certainly satirises Frank Chin's brand of
cultural nationalism through the figure of Wittman at times,
such as in this section:

He had been tripping out on the wrong side of the street.
The wrong side of the world. What had he to do with
foreigners? With F.O.B. émigrés? Fifth-generation native
Californian that he was. Great-Great-Grandfather came
on the *Nootka*, as ancestral as the Mayflower. Go-sei.
(*TM*, p. 41)

Chin's *über*-masculinity, that he sees as an expression of an
Asian heroic tradition, is re-inscribed by Kingston in the gentler,
more sensitive figure of Wittman. In *Tripmaster Monkey*, too,

Kingston's use of 'fakery' is consciously and specifically woven into the meaning of the novel. In interviews, Kingston has described her particular use of the term 'fake':

> That's a jazz term. Jazz musicians used to compile a book of basic tunes, songs, chords. Sometimes it would be just the beginning of a tune, then they would improvise. I was trying to write a prose book with basic plots, suggestions for social action, for trips – I hope to trip the reader out and then improvise further.[58]

A 'fake book', then, is the guide book of basic melodies that jazz musicians use when improvising. Kingston's 'fake books' in *Tripmaster* comprise the Chinese dynastic novels that I have discussed, and the many intertextual allusions to novels and stories that she incorporates into the narrative. Some are more obviously present than others: James Joyce's *Ulysses* provides both plot fodder and a style to improvise upon, as Wittman's trail around the Bay Area echoes Leopold Bloom's literal and mental wanderings; archetypal stories of the struggle for union and community such as *Romeo and Juliet* and *West Side Story* contribute to Wittman's dream of making *communitas*; and Walt Whitman's exuberant imaginings in *Song of Myself* are re-inscribed in Wittman's free-form trip-vision. The 'fake book' not only provides Kingston with a means to formally recycle inherited myths and stories, though; it also enables her to foreground the processes of improvisation as narrative technique, as she describes it here:

> In my book, as Witman [sic] gathers his troupe, he gives them – and my readers – many ideas for plays, poems, jokes, epics, novels – a literature, a theater. ... So I hope to let Witman give away plots, characters, ideas, and thus Chinese Americans – and others, of course – who read this book can use it for a fake book.[59]

As Debra Shostak also observes in her influential reading of *Tripmaster Monkey* in 'Maxine Hong Kingston's Fake Books', Kingston's trademark blend of Chinese and American cultural artefacts and styles is also evident here in her use of the form of *hua-pen*, prompt books used by professional Chinese story-tellers in the series recitals of their epics. Shostak notes that *'Hua-pen* would typically include the major episodes of a traditional story, but storytellers were known for adding new episodes in their recitations' and remarks that 'the improvisational nature of both telling and writing down the classic stories is clear'.[60] In this sense, then, as Shostak argues, Kingston's very style *becomes* that of the fake book, in an ironic end-game move in the Frank Chin–Maxine Hong Kingston controversy.

Wittman's rant: counteracting stereotypes

> It has to do with looks, doesn't it? They use 'American' interchangeably with 'white'. The clean-cut all-American look. This hairless body … is cleaner than most. I bathe, I dress up; all I get is soo mun and sah chun. (Maxine Hong Kingston, *Tripmaster Monkey: His Fake Book*, p. 329)

> quite often I feel forced to write against the stereotype (Maxine Hong Kingston, interview with Shelley Fisher Fishkin)[61]

In 1981, writing of her plans for *Tripmaster Monkey*, Kingston wrote that 'I want to work with the following challenges: What is the identity of the Chinese American today? Is there anything besides looks that distinguishes us from other Americans?'[62] These were not simply idle musings, but represented the culmination of Kingston's frustration with the racism she had encountered as a Chinese American writer. As other chapters document, Kingston has suffered from repeated misreadings of her work in a racist vein. *Tripmaster Monkey* culminates in an extensive rant against racism and stereotyping, two of the many evils identified in the novel. 'One Man Show', the final episode, opens with Wittman announcing to both his play's audience and his readers: 'I want to talk to you' (*TM*, p. 307), and then proceeds into thirty pages of barely controlled invective. As Elaine Kim and other critics have shown, ethnic stereotyping has continued to be a regrettable feature across the range of forms of representation in American culture. Writers like Kingston have thus inherited a tradition of representing Asian Americans encumbered by such images. In her key essay 'Ethnic Subject, Ethnic Sign, and the Difficulty of Rehabilitative Representation: Chinatown in Some Works of Chinese American Fiction', Sauling Wong asks: 'when subject and sign have both been altered by the gaze of white society, how is a Chinese American writer to represent his/her own experiences?'[63] This is Kingston's – and Wittman's – dilemma in *Tripmaster Monkey*: how exactly to write – right – a rehabilitative representation of the Asian American subject? Wong's analysis draws upon semiology to explore the process of representing (and misrepresenting) Chinatown. She uses William Boelhower's work on ethnic semiosis[64] to suggest that the 'cultural product' of Chinatown (that is, the dominant cultural image of Chinatown) is created by a process of joint semiosis, in which the gaze of the dominator and the dominated (the white and the ethnic subject respectively) engage in a 'process of mutual constitution' to represent Chinatown.[65] Wong notes that this mutual semiosis/gaze 'hardly implies equal partnership',[66] because the gaze of the ethnic subject is economically and discursively less powerful than that of the white subject. Wong's analysis of this process shows us that for the ethnic subject *self*-representation is not always possible, precisely because the 'gaze of white society dominates', and as she notes 'the "Chinaman" no longer fully owns his experiences'.[67] The question is one of how exactly to divorce ethnic self-representation from the debilitating images with which it has been saddled? Wong argues that because of the potency of the white gaze, the ethnic subject is 'now *marked* ... singled out, blemished'.[68] The ramification of the racist white gaze is thus that ethnic self-representation becomes highly problematic and fraught with near-insurmountable difficulty:

> the Orientalising sign may become so pervasive and invasive as to monopolise all expression. When that happens, the subjectivity of the ethnic subject is in danger of being drained from any effort at self representation.[69]

Consequently, the ethnic subject often lacks agency to control self-representation. Moreover, because the racist white gaze 'marks' the ethnic subject as ethnic, 'other', the body itself may become the dominant signifier of representation. Thus, being caught in the racialising gaze of another can constitute a crisis of self and of self-representation. Wittman frequently refers to this in his *Tripmaster* diatribes, often describing how he becomes entangled with the racialising gaze whereby individual characteristics, responses and features are erased, or remain unseen, because as an ethnic subject he signifies only otherness, difference. In such situations, the possibilities for interpersonal engagements disappear, as the racialising gaze obliterates the identity and signifying canvas of the other. As Sau-ling Wong writes: 'The gaze of cultural voyeurs effectively "disappears" the people: every Chinese in its sight is reduced to a specimen of Otherness devoid of individuality and interiority'.[70]

Stereotypes comprise some of the most deeply rooted elements of racist representation, and hence any rehabilitative project thus necessitates finding ways to escape stereotypical self-images. Counteractive measures are difficult, however, because the process of racist stereotyping is inextricably linked to the preservation of racial hierarchies, as Elaine Kim observes:

> Stereotypes of racial minorities are a record of prejudices; they are part of an attempt to justify various attitudes and practices. The function of stereotypes of Asians in Anglo-American literature has been to provide literary rituals through which myths of white racial supremacy might be continually reaffirmed.[71]

Such stereotypes are highly durable, not only in cultural media, where, as Joseph Rothschild suggests in his study *Ethnopolitics*, 'stereotypes … become psychologically useful, and hence highly resistant to correction',[72] but also in the individual conscious-ness; as Amy Ling notes stereotypes are 'based on fixed concepts within the perceiver's head'.[73]

Wittman's treatise, which closes *Tripmaster Monkey*, is perhaps the most lengthy indictment of racist stereotyping in

Asian American literature to date.[74] Here, Wittman covers, over several pages, the whole gamut of his preoccupations with racism, with especial emphasis on the processes involved in stereotyping. Wittman discusses inscrutability ('we're not inscrutable at all'); the emasculation of the Asian male ('two parts of the anatomy that are deficient in orientals. The nose and the penis'); cultural stereotyping ('I'm warning you, you ask me about food shit, I'll recommend a dog-shit restaurant'); as well as linguistic stereotypes ('They expect us to go into our Charlie Chan Fu Manchu act … They … are cutting off our balls linguistically. "Me no likee"') (*TM*, p. 310; p. 329). He goes on to discuss filmic misrepresentations of Asians at length, and to point out the inaccuracy of such representations:

> A racist movie is always running on some channel. Just the other night, I saw another one that kills off the Chinese guy … he talks to himself, rubbing his hands together, plotting, 'I will convert a missionary.' Which is racially and religiously very fucked up. Chinese don't convert white people but vice versa. (*TM* pp. 320–321)

Through Wittman's exegesis on racist stereotyping we see Kingston engaging with and refuting various stereotypes that work to categorise Asian American women and men. In particular, Wittman attacks the highly sexualised and exoticised stereotypical image of the Asian female and answers the question 'Is it true about these Oriental women'; '"The full line," interrupts Wittman, "is, 'Is it true what they say about Chinese girls' twats?' They think they're sideways, that they slant like eyes"' (*TM*, p. 317). Wittman continues with the connection between physiognomy and stereotyping:

> They want to hear me answer something obscene, something bodily. Some disgusting admission about our anatomy. About daikon legs and short waist or long waist, and that the twat goes sideways, slanting like her eyes. They want me to show them the Mongoloidian spot on my ass. They want to measure the length of my ape arms and compare them to Negers' arms. (*TM*, p. 317)

I *am* this tall. I didn't get this tall by being experimented on by scientists trying to find the secret of height. They're looking for a time hormone in the pituitary gland; maybe the chronons are up there. Speeding them up (or slowing them down) may fool the body into growing more. They're taking unused time from the brains of cadavers and injecting it into the brains of short little orientals. (*TM*, pp. 328–329)

He describes stereotypes thus: '"I think," he tried explaining, "that history being trapped in people means that history is embodied in physical characteristics"' (*TM*, p. 312), thereby drawing attention to the tendency to draw conclusions about groups of people from assumed shared physiognomy, and he then homes in on the racist tendency to try to 'read' the body:

And do you know what part of our bodies they find so mysteriously inscrutable? It's our little eyes. They think they can't see into these little squinny eyes. They think we're sneaky, squinnying at them through spy eyes. They can't see inside here past these slits. (*TM*, p. 312)

For the benefit of the reader or listener guilty of such assumptions, he finally notes:

Take a good look at these eyes … it's an American face. Notice as I profile, you can see both my eyes at once. I see more than most people – no bridge that blocks the view between the eyes. I have a wide-angle windshield. Take a good look. These are the type of eyes most preferred for the movies … these are movie star eyes. (*TM*, p. 315)

Wittman's assault on physiognomic racism here is very astute. At the same time as refuting stereotypes about vision, the body and other matters, Wittman invites the reader or listener to appraise him in a voyeuristic, quasi-anthropological manner, a manoeuvre which simultaneously reproduces and condemns such actions. Then Wittman deals with practice on the part of certain Asian American women to resort to cosmetic surgery in order to change their looks:

And that's why you girls are slicing your eyelids open, isn't it? Poor girls. I understand. And you glue on the false eyelashes to give your scant eyes some definition … I have been requesting my actresses to take off their false eyelashes, to go on bare-face and show what we look like. I promise, they will find a new beauty. But every one of them draw on eyeliner, top and bottom rims, and also up here on the bone to make like deep sockets. Then mascara, then-clamp, clamp. They kink their stubby lashes with this metal pincher that looks like a metal plow. With spirit gum and tape, they glue on a couple of rows per eye of fake-hair falsies. A bulge of fat swells out over the tape-a crease, a fold-allthesame Caucasoid … Worse than make-up … is the eye operation … You girls shouldn't do that to yourselves. It's supposed to make you more attractive to men, right? Speaking as a man, I don't want to kiss eyes that have been cut and sewn; I'd be thinking Bride of Frankenstein. But I guess you're not trying to attract my type. I can tell when somebody's had her lids done. After she gets her stitches pulled and the puffiness goes down, she doesn't have a fold exactly, it's a scar line across each roundish lid. And her mien has been like lifted. Like she ate something too hot. The jalapeño look. She'll have to meet new guys who will believe she was born like that. She'll draw black lines on top of the scars, and date white guys, who don't care one way or the other single-lid double-lid. (*TM*, pp. 312–313)

Kingston's voice, as the omniscient narrator, interrupts Wittman's monologue at this point to note that:

Several pioneer showgirls were present who had secretly had that operation done long ago. They were laughing at the girl with the jalapeño expression. They did not admit that all you have to do is leave your eyes alone, and grow old; the lids will naturally develop a nice wrinkle. (*TM*, p. 313)

The irony at this point is searing, and overall, Wittman's rant functions as a powerful assault upon a matrix of racism and stereotyping, and is therefore an apposite way to close the novel. Part of the success of Kingston's potent indictment of stereotyping at the end of the text is due to her use of Wittman Ah Sing as her spokesperson. His up-beat, off-centre and slightly crazed perspective invigorates the condemnation of stereo-typing. Wittman's narrative stance as purveyor of an eclectic array of cultural snippets enables him to switch between stereo-typical representations with a fluidity which adds momentum to his rage against racism, as well as his – and Kingston's – anti-establishment politics and imbrication in the ethos of the sixties' counterculture.

Writing place – the politics of locality:
Hawai'i One Summer (1987/1998)

> What thick novels I could brood up here with no inter-
> rupting chapter breaks but one long thought from front to
> back cover. (*Hawai'i One Summer*, p. 3)[1]

> It may be here that one can best sense the impact on
> Kingston of fame and prominence, the payoff and the price
> of parting the black curtains of silence. (Diane Simmons,
> *Maxine Hong Kingston*, p. 22)

Published in the wake of her first literary success, but reissued
in 1988, *Hawai'i One Summer* reminds us of Kingston's strong
attachment to place: here the Hawai'i of her early married years,
where she worked as a teacher, raised her son and wrote her first
fiction. A series of occasional pieces, the writing in *Hawai'i One
Summer* is at times elegiac, nostalgic, and pensive, but often also
exuberant and a sincere celebration of what Kingston regards as
the timelessness of a landscape and culture too often regarded as
little more than an American holiday resort, or rural Pacific
idyll. Together the pieces reflect upon Kingston's commitment
to the Hawai'ian islands, at first as a sojourner then as a resident,
and articulate the importance of a matrix of place, community,
'belonging' and the 'local', both in Hawai'i and as represented,
here and elsewhere, in Kingston's writing. *Hawai'i One Summer*
also bears testimony to another dimension of Kingston's work
which has hitherto gone unrecognised. As an extensive meditation upon place and environment in Hawai'i, the pieces here
together represent Kingston's imbrication in a politics of

ecology, and specifically a form of ecological feminism as well. Thus, I argue in this chapter that *Hawai'i One Summer* warrants – indeed demands – critical attention as providing an additional, previously unconsidered, perspective upon this renowned writer.

Maxine moved to Hawai'i with her husband Earll and their young son, Joseph, in 1967, 'in despair' as Kingston remembers in 'War' (*HOS*, p. 15). Initially this move was intended to escape the Vietnam War and the draft, but, as the Kingstons found to their dismay, this was less than easy: 'Hawai'i had its own problems, and with the presence of the military here, the Vietnam War was even more real on these islands', Kingston remembers,[2] and in fact 'we had not, of course, escaped from the war, but had put ourselves in the very midst of it, as close as you could get and remain in the United States' ('War', *HOS*, p. 16). Or as she writes in the Preface to the 1998 edition:

> A black cloud had covered my home place, Northern California. But leaving the mainland for Hawai'i had not gotten us out from under it. The black pall that spread over the world during the long war had not lifted. In 1978, the year of the Summer of this book, I was continuing my depression from the Vietnam War. The fallout from that war went on and on – wars in Cambodia and Laos, MIAs, agent orange, boat people. (*HOS*, p. xi)

In retrospect though, Kingston acknowledges that she and Earll were misguided in thinking that Hawai'i would allow an escape from the war: 'We should have thought of it – hardware and soldiers were sent to Hawai'i' ('War', *HOS*, p. 16), she says.

Hawai'i One Summer comprises eleven prose pieces, written in 1978, during the summer months from June to August, and was originally published in 1987 by Meadow Press as a small hand-set run of 150 copies, crafted of paper from the Kozo rice fields in Korea, together with original woodblock prints by the Taoist teacher and son of the well-known Chinese American author Jade Snow Wong, Deng Ming-Dao, and which sold for $400–$500 each ('Preface', *HOS*, pp. xv–xvi). Originally, many of the prose pieces were written for Kingston's 'Hers' column which was published in the *New York Times*, as diary entries, where Kingston had decided to 'write personally, about myself'.[3] As *Hawai'i One Summer* the pieces were collectively later republished by the University of Hawai'i Press, and through this reached a much wider readership. Thus, three separate historical moments inform and influence the text. The pieces are heavily imbued with Kingston's unease at the Vietnam War and both its geo-political and environmental effects, and this is clearly reflective of her early years on the islands. The period in which she actually composed the pieces, the mid-1970s, is evident in her repeated meditations upon both war (how to avoid it) and peace (how to promote it), the fairly carefree existence she had here in Hawai'i, her attempt to live in a politically conscious manner, including her rejection of material possessions ('no petty talk about material things' she declares on page 3), the relationship between her writing and education, and the importance of roots, a sense of belonging and of home.[4] Finally, it should be noted that the republication of the text ten years later by the University of Hawai'i Press occurred after Kingston had achieved significant prominence internationally, and this casts many of the pieces in a new light, as the epigraphal comment by Diane Simmons suggests.

'Aina', Hawai'i and the politics of the 'local'

At the heart of the collection, though, stands Kingston's abiding admiration for the Hawai'ian people's celebration of place. In Hawai'i, place is linked very strongly to the community, and the celebration of the culture of the community. Kingston notes: 'Hawai'ians have a sense of the community and the tribe ... along with the music and the mythology'[5] which is linked to place:

> The sense of place has to do with everything. ... abstract ideas and values are nothing. They're invisible, they're not dramatic, and they're not interesting unless you can localize them.[6]

In recent years it has become fashionable in literary criticism and critical theory to speak of a politics of the 'local' as central to the study of ethnic, 'marginalised' or 'regional' literatures, partly in opposition to 'global' influences, or the encroachment of globalisation via big businesses and other interventions.[7] But Kingston's conception of place and the 'local' here has less to do with the fashionable currents of critical theory, and more to do with keying into the culturally specific traditions of Hawai'i itself. In more general critical usage, the 'local', along with cognate terms such as the 'regional', as Miranda Joseph observes, 'have to do with *place* ... but often metamorphose into connoting social *spaces* that do not correlate with place – kinship, ethnicity, culture, or community'.[8] But as Stephen Sumida tells us, 'in Hawai'i's island culture, *place* is conceived as *history*'.[9] Kingston expresses this particular usage through her description of the concept of *aina*, or what we might translate as 'land-spirit-people':

> I feel that my years in Hawai'i taught me a lot about local habitation in many senses. In the Hawai'ian language and in Hawai'i, there's a word, *aina*. It's a common word, it's part of the state motto that we respect the *aina*. A simple English translation for it is 'the land.' But it's more than the land because when you talk about *aina*, you also talk about the spirit of the people. So this is very political. We're talking about native peoples who believe that a human being is alive because of a relationship with the land. The land has a spirit, it has energy and power and we grow out of it, like trees. When the people lose the land, they die.[10]

As with *aina*, the sense of the 'local' also has a specific usage in Hawai'i, as Kingston explains:

> As I say that word – 'local' – that's really another political word in Hawai'i. A 'local' is a person who looks like me. It's a fight against colonialism. ... When you're colonized, it means that they take away your local stories, your local customs, your local identity – take away your land, your *aina*. This is why all the surfer kids, when they say they're local, fight for their surfing spots, calling them local. The forces against being local are immense – urbanization, the wiping out of talk-stories by the print culture and the

television culture, wiping out the myths.[11]

It is for this reason that Kingston felt herself to be an outsider (that is, *not* local), for many years on the islands, as she describes:

> In Hawai'i I was always a stranger. The Hawai'ian culture cultivates that. Because the Hawai'ians are a beleaguered people, or a colonized people, they make up all kinds of defences. And I think one of the defences is that they have a wonderful secret culture that is the heart of Hawai'i.[12]

And in 1979 she observed that 'this is a hard place to belong to'.[13] It was eventually through Maxine's son, Joseph, that she found a sense of belonging: 'My son likes Hawai'i very much. It's his home. Even though Earll and I don't have Hawai'ian blood, I can see that Joseph is a Hawai'ian person', she observed,[14] and acknowledged that 'Hawai'ians have a sense of the community and the tribe, which has become his, along with the music and the mythology'.[15] In the Preface to *Hawai'i One Summer* Kingston describes in detail her awareness of the acuteness of a politics of place within the islands:

> The literary community in Hawai'i argues over who owns the myths and stories, whether the local language and writings should be exported to the Mainland, whether so-and-so is authentic, is Hawai'ian. For me, Hawai'i was a good place for writing about California and China, and not for writing about Hawai'i. I felt the kapu – these are not your stories to write; these myths are not your myths; the Hawai'ians are not your people. You are haole. You are katonk. My great grandfathers, one on my mother's side, one on my father's side, and my paternal grandfather lived and worked in Hawai'i. Even so, they were not kama'āina, and I am not kama'āina. (*HOS*, p. xii)

Kingston's sense of the hostile boundaries protecting 'local' Hawai'ian culture – she describes it as '*kapu*', or taboo – is very strong here. This clashes with her own sense of herself as an insider by way of her ancestral history, yet she, like her grand-parents before her, nevertheless remains externally designated as something of an outsider, not 'kama'āina', a quite charged

Hawai'ian term which translates as 'native'. Hawai'ian Asian American critic Stephen Sumida has discussed the politics of the 'local' in Hawai'i at some length in his study of Hawai'ian literatures, *And the View From the Shore: Literary Traditions of Hawai'i*. The designation 'local', he asserts, may refer to a whole spectrum of subject positions, including 'native Hawai'ian, colonial, tourist, and polyethnic local literatures'.[16] Here, he expands upon the particular problematics of its definition:

> The term 'local,' as in 'local-style' food, culture, T-shirts, or 'whatevah,' has been used so much that a backlash has developed against it and the people it describes – a backlash that is still loudly evident … A 'local' (meaning here a certain kind of person) is usually thought of as nonwhite, for instance a native Hawai'ian, Asian American, Samoan, or Puerto Rican; or a local may be someone historically, ethnically originating in the working classes of Hawai'i. … An Asian American newcomer … could choose to blend into a local ethnicity – that is, to pass for being local-born … a newcomer to Hawai'i becomes a 'local' when he or she considers him or herself a participating member of Hawai'i's society.[17]

as well as the sensitivities such a term keys into:

> local is today's shorthand by which people in Hawai'i – whether local or not, whether in pride or in derision – label a culture, a sensibility, an identity, and, often forgotten despite how strongly it is valued, a personal, family, and community history. Local culture in Hawai'i has its own rituals, codes, and sensibilities.[18]

Sumida goes even further in his later, 1997, essay, 'Post-colonialism, Nationalism, and the Emergence of Asian/Pacific American Literatures', when he speaks of 'Asian American locals' (p. 277).[19] In fact, as Rachel Lee defines it, 'local' literature is actually distinct from either mainland continental Asian American literature or Hawai'ian literature, since the first category is a 'mainland' construction (as opposed to 'from the shore') and the second implies native Hawai'ian.[20] Another very useful definition of 'local' literature is offered by Darrell Lum and

Eric Chock, two Hawai'ian Asian American writers, who describe it as having: 'a distinct sensitivity to ethnicity, the environment (in particular the land), a sense of personal lineage and family history, and the use of the sound, the languages, and the vocabulary of island people'.[21] So can we describe Kingston as 'local', and *Hawai'i One Summer* as a 'local' text? Clearly Kingston remains a writer predominantly of and concerned with the continental United States; yet here in *Hawai'i One Summer* we can see her almost complete identification with the politics, and what we could term the positionalities or localities, of Hawai'ian culture and environment. There is undoubtedly a strong sense of Hawai'i's *locale* in the text as well. And as Deborah Madsen has noted, although Kingston originally intended to largely leave out a consideration of Hawai'i in these essays, in actual fact, this is precisely what she has achieved:

> Kingston wrote about California and China, about experiences that were personal to her and her family. But still Hawai'i enters the essays, in the descriptions of the sea, air and landscapes, and in the history that determines the quality of contemporary life in Hawai'i.[22]

One recurrent feature of 'local' writing in Hawai'i is the attempt to write against a history of external definition, stereotyping through popular images of Hawai'i as a rural idyll, and historical colonial interference, or what have together been termed a 'tourist' influence.[23] Kingston can be seen here in this collection of essays to adopt an 'anti-tourist' perspective in her depiction of island culture and place, as well as her abhorrence of American imperialist military presence on the islands, with the accompanying territorial encroachments upon the Hawai'ian people. Her work is in fact very reminiscent of some other Hawai'ian 'local' writers, such as Gary Pak and Sylvia Watanabe, in this respect (see for instance, Pak's story 'The Watcher of Waipuna' and Watanabe's celebrated 1991 novel *Talking to the Dead*).

Hawai'i One Summer as ecotext

> Describing Nature, the sea, the air, the lands and fish, is describing Hawai'i. (*HOS*, p. xiii)

> The householder is only one incarnation away from snail or turtle or kangaroo. (*HOS*, p. 3)

As we saw above, 'local' writing encompasses a heightened sensitivity to both land and environment. In the opening essay of the collection, 'Our First House', Kingston declares: 'I don't need to own land to belong to this planet' *(HOS*, p. 3). Of the eleven pieces that comprise the text, five are explicitly about Kingston's relationship with the land and with the nature which surrounds her and her family: 'Our First House', 'Chinaman's Hat', 'A City Person Encountering Nature', 'Strange Sightings' and 'A Sea Worry'. These are also interspersed with four evocative black and white photographs of places of significance in the Hawai'ian Islands: Lana'i, Hawai'i; Manoa Valley, Honolulu; Chinaman's Hat, O'ahu; and the Big Island, Hawai'i. Although it is probably not a label that Kingston would choose to use, much of the writing in *Hawai'i One Summer* might be conceived of as a form of ecofeminism. Described by the veteran ecocritic and eco-activist Ynestra King as the 'third wave of the women's movement', ecofeminism is defined as 'a politics which combines feminism, environmentalism, antiracism, animal rights, anti-imperialism, antimilitarism' – or, in other words, a summary of Kingston's many intertwined political stances.[24] In fact, as Noël Sturgeon argues in her essay 'The Nature of Race', ecofeminism is an apposite way to describe an interconnected set of political beliefs which started with antimilitarism, which is so central to Kingston's credo:

> Many women involved in ... antimilitarist direct actions ... began calling themselves ecofeminists in the middle eighties as a way of describing their interlocking political concerns.[25]

Maria Mies describes the emergence of ecofeminism as a historically specific event as well:

Ecofeminism ... grew out of various social movements –
the feminist, peace and the ecology movements – in the
late 1970s and early 1980s[26]

so, in other words, co-terminously with the writing of the pieces
that comprise *Hawai'i One Summer*. In what ways, then, might
we think of these pieces in *Hawai'i One Summer* as ecofeminist? Gretchen T. Legler has discussed some features of
ecofeminist creative writing, and suggests that women writers
of ecofeminist literature 'image ... human/nature relationships
as "conversations" between knowing subjects' and that the project of ecofeminist writing is '"remything" nature as a speaking,
"bodied" subject' in 'a relationship of friendship and care'.[27] In
the light of these descriptions, let us pause to consider one of the
key nature essays in *Hawai'i One Summer*, 'A City Person
Encountering Nature'. Viewed through the lens of the above comments on ecofeminist endeavour, this piece emerges as quintessentially ecofeminist in orientation. The essay describes Kingston's
dawning awareness of the powerful presence of nature in her
surroundings and her gradual shift from a position of neutral
observer of natural phenomena to a caring participant in an
exchange of sensory perception with her natural environment.
Initially, she expresses her disregard for nature as a city person:

A city person encountering nature hardly recognizes it,
has no patience for its cycles, and disregards animals and
plants unless they roar and exfoliate in spectacular
aberrations. Preferring the city myself, I can better discern
natural phenomena when books point them out; I also
need to verify what I think I've seen, even though charts
of phyla and species are orderly whereas nature is wild,
unruly. (*HOS*, p. 35)

The essay then proceeds to a re-evaluation of Kingston's interaction with natural phenomena. The majority of the piece con-
sists of an extended description of a period during the preceding
summer (the essay appears in the 'July' chapter), when Kingston
and her friend spent three days together at a beach cottage, and
rose early together each day to see what 'critters' (*HOS*, p. 36)

the ocean had washed up. Kingston describes the human-like behaviour of what turn out to be 'nudibranchs' in intimate and extended detail. She goes on to speak more generally of the wonders of nature, and refers to her various encounters with ants, giant mushrooms, and philodendrons, as well as other documents of a series of random wondrous natural phenomena – a stampede of cows, a snake discovered inside another snake, an alligator imbibing a pigeon, and other incidents, as she describes:

> I've watched ants make off with a used Band-Aid. I've watched a single termite bore through a book, a circle clean through. I saw a pigeon vomit milk, and didn't know whether it was sick, or whether its babies had died and the milk sacs in its throat were engorged. I have a friend who was pregnant at the same time as her mare, and, just exactly like the Chinese superstition that only one of the babies would live, the horse gave birth to a foal in two pieces. (*HOS*, p. 39)

These descriptions are set alongside references to literary homages to nature in all of its power and glory, such as William Blake's 'Tyger, Tyger' and Stevens's 'Thirteen Ways of Looking at a Blackbird'. In juxtaposition with such pieces, Kingston's evocation of sea-nature emerges as a eulogistic celebration of both place and species. Ultimately, Kingston reaches a point at the end of this lengthy description where she is able to say that 'a new climate helps me to see nature' (*HOS*, p. 37).

Many elements of the piece echo the descriptions of eco-feminist literature as described by Gretchen T. Legler above. Creatures of nature are not only anthropomorphised but named (Kingston's son has a pet crab named 'Linda'); the connection between humanity and nature is emphasised through suggesting a conversational interchange between Kingston, her friend and the nature they observe, and the boundary between the two is eroded; and so the essay also ultimately reinscribes the natural as super-natural, as having quasi-mythical qualities. The collection contains several other essays in an ecofeminist vein, too, notably 'Chinaman's Hat', which immediately precedes 'A City Person Encountering Nature', so these two pieces function together as an eco-diptych.

Another hallmark of ecofeminist literature is its willingness to explore different dimensions of spirituality and mythology, a preoccupation we find too in *Hawai'i One Summer*. A further manifestation of Kingston's fascination with place, nature and landscape in this collection is to be found in the ninth essay, 'Strange Sightings'. Here, Kingston explores the metaphysical dimensions of the Hawai'ian islands' landscape, and the interconnection between land and mythology. Hawai'i, it turns out, is especially rich territory for the inhabitation of spirits and the propagation of mythical elements described in the opening sections:

> According to mystical people, spiritual forces converge at Hawai'i, as do ocean currents and winds. Kahuna, keepers and teachers of the old religion and arts (such as song writing, the hula, navigation, taro growing), still work here. ... Some kahuna say they see tree spirits fly from branch to branch; the various winds and rains are spirits too; sharks and rocks have spirits. If ancestors and immortals travel on supernatural errands between China and the Americas, they must rest here in transit. (*HOS*, p. 53)

It is common in the collection as a whole for Kingston to refer to the very land of Hawai'i as being, literally, *super*-natural, as she does here in this essay too:

> Hawai'i, new land which has recently risen out of the water, has overwhelming animism; that is, it seems more alive than cities which have been paved over for hundreds of years. ... Even our friends with Ph.Ds see things in Hawai'i. Our friend from Minnesota kept telling us about the row of fishermen walking in the ocean with torches at night. 'They're chanting to attract the fish,' he said. Later, he learned he was describing the march of the dead warriors. (*HOS*, p. 54)[28]

Kingston also describes her own experience of seeing spirits: 'I saw a whirling witch in the intersection by our house. She had one red cheek and one black cheek. Surrounded by a screaming, pointing cloud, she turned and turned on her broom' (*HOS*, p. 54), and also many other 'strange sightings' reported by her husband, son and friends.

Re-negotiating 'local' literature: the 1978 'talk-story' conference

As the above discussion attests, the prominent preoccupation in *Hawai'i One Summer* is Kingston's relationship with Hawai'i, which is also linked to her role as a writer. The most fulsome exploration of this preoccupation is to be found in the ninth piece, 'Talk Story: A Writers' Conference'. This was Hawai'i's first ethnic American writers' conference, held in 1978, which convened to explore the presence of Asian American literature in the islands' culture, and came to define Hawai'i's sense of its own literature for the coming few decades. The conference has subsequently been remembered as quite notorious, as well as being a pivotal moment in the self-definition of Hawai'i's literary community. Kingston recalls her unease with some of the discussions held at the conference:

> Listening to the keynote speakers the next morning, I was humbled when Ozzie Bushnell, author of *Ka'a'awa*, said that if 'us local kids' don't write the Hawai'i novel, then 'the outsider' will come in and do it. I guiltily identified with this 'outsider.' Ozzie is such a strong speaker, talking both standard English and pidgin, that I felt scolded, a Captain Cook of literature, plundering the islands for metaphors, looting images, distorting the landscape with a mainland – a mainstream – viewpoint. (*HOS*, p. 47)

Kingston's discomfort connects with her own vexed status as part-insider, part-outsider in Hawai'i. In 1978 the term 'Asian Pacific American' was innovative, and, as with all such labels, triggered as much rejection as identification; as Kingston remembers 'many people denied every term in it' (*HOS*, p. xii). For Kingston, the conference crystallised the many interconnected concerns of locality, belonging and creativity she had grappled with since her arrival:

> We were divided between those who would give the stories, myths, ceremonies to whoever hears them, and those who would have possession be by blood. I decided ... I ... would bypass Hawai'i. I meant to honor kapu, not touch kapu things at all. (*HOS*, p. xiii)

Critic Diane Simmons sums up the significance of the conference for Kingston:

> Kingston can be glimpsed attempting to find a silver lining
> in the controversial conference ... Writing recently of that
> conference in a re-issued edition ... Kingston recalls a
> general tone of conflict over the question of who owns
> stories.[29]

An alternative record of the events of this conference can be
found in Asian American Hawai'ian academic, Stephen Sumida's
1991 book, *And the View From the Shore*:

> O. A. Bushnell delivered the keynote address ... [and]
> challenged [the] assumption that there is no Asian
> American literature of Hawai'i ... Historically, Hawai'i
> has had any number of visiting writers ... the image of the
> visiting writer in Hawai'i is of an artist retreating from
> urban, mainland America to the balm of the islands.[30]

Kingston's Hawai'i: *The Woman Warrior* and *China Men*

This debate on belonging, ownership, exclusion and literary
production prefigures, of course, the intense scrutiny Kingston's
work was to receive across the water in California a decade later
when she was viciously attacked, in 1984 and 1991 respectively,
by the Chinese American writer Frank Chin for the 'fakery' of
her writing in *The Woman Warrior*; for her failure, as Chin saw
it, to pay necessary homage to the indigenous traditions of
Chinese America and instead to publish a narrative which 'violated
beyond recognition' the myths and stories of 'her' culture.[31] Yet
as the reflections of *Hawai'i One Summer* attest, Kingston had
already devoted much time and thought to the question of what
we might term the 'ethnic ethics' of literary production.
Kingston's decision in her life-writing volumes *The Woman
Warrior* and *China Men* to blend mythical and literary modes
reflects her conclusion in *Hawai'i One Summer* that the best

way to avoid the kinds of controversy displayed at the 'Talk Story' conference was to 'bypass' (*HOS*, p. xii) contention entirely. Since she tried to 'honor kapu, not touch kapu things at all' (ibid.) but finally 'realize[d] a way free to tell a story' (*HOS*, p. xiii) we can assume that personally, at least, Kingston had resolved the dilemma of authorial freedom long before the 'pen wars' with Frank Chin erupted. In the final analysis, it appears ironic that the very feature of Kingston's writing for which she was so condemned: her mixed-genre, episodic style, has in fact been the distinctive hallmark of all of her writing from the early pieces in *Hawai'i One Summer* onwards.

Kingston lived in Hawai'i between 1967 and 1984. The majority of the essays in the collection were written co-terminously with Kingston's life-writing volume, *China Men*, which was published in 1980. In many ways, *Hawai'i One Summer* functions as a co-text to *China Men*, which serves to offer a new perspective upon this book as well. Usually read as a historiographic metafiction about Kingston's male ancestors, *China Men* has generally been evaluated as a slightly less accomplished version of the life story she tells in *The Woman Warrior*. Yet, by juxtaposing *China Men* with *Hawai'i One Summer*, a more complex narrative emerges in which the braiding together of place and history, as well as ancestry, can be found. Kingston describes the connection between the two books:

> I was finishing *China Men* in the summer when other people were vacationing. So, for breaks, I wrote these pieces. But I was in the world of *China Men*, and its images kept appearing everywhere – in my letters to friends, in life, and in this book. So, here again, are the frigate birds in the air currents, creatures on the beach, assembly lines funneling napalm to Vietnam, the sandalwood that was still here in Hawai'i when my great-grandfathers came. (*HOS*, p. xviii)

The second section of *China Men*, entitled 'The Great Grandfather of the Sandalwood Mountains', relates the history of Kingston's great-grandfather, Bak Goong, who travelled to Hawai'i. Kingston imaginatively reconstructs her grandfather's story as he lived and worked in the Sandalwood Mountains. As

I discuss further in the chapter on *China Men*, here we can see the influence Hawai'i as place has had upon this book:

> I have gone east, that is, west, as far as Hawai'i, where I have stood alongside the highway at the edge of the sugar-cane and listened for the voices of the great grandfathers. ... Driving along O'ahu's windward side, where sugarcane grew in my great grandfather's day, I like looking out at the ocean.[32]

This quotation leads into an extensive description of Kingston's experience swimming out to the so-called Chinaman's Hat, her encounter with various forms of sea life on the way, and her feelings of synchronicity with nature when she arrives. This description bears striking similarity to the ecofeminist key of 'A City Person Encountering Nature'. I quote it at length in order to illustrate this:

> I swam out to Chinaman's Hat. We walked partway in low tide, then put on face masks. Once you open your eyes in the water, you become a flying creature. Schools of fish – zebra fish, rainbow fish, red fish – curve with the currents, swim alongside and away; balloon fish puff out their porcupine quills. How unlike a dead fish a live fish is. We swam through spangles of silver-white fish, their scales like sequins. Sometimes we entered cold spots, deserts, darkness under clouds, where the sand churned like grey fog, and sometimes we entered golden chambers. There are summer forests and winter forests down there. Sea cucumbers, holothurians, rocked side to side. A sea turtle glided by and that big shell is no encumbrance in the water. ... I have heard the land sing. I have seen the bright blue streaks of spirits whisking through the air. I again search for my American ancestors by listening in the cane.[33]

In this section of *China Men*, Kingston establishes an atavistic connection to her male ancestors via establishing an intimacy with the places and spaces of Hawai'i. As in *Hawai'i One Summer* there is no gap in the envisioning of human, spirit, nature and land; instead these are figured as part of a seamless continuum.

The Fifth Book of Peace (2003)
and To Be the Poet (2002)

The images of peace are ephemeral. The language of peace is subtle. The reasons for peace, the definitions of peace, the very idea of peace have to be invented, and invented again. (Epilogue, *The Fifth Book of Peace*, p. 402)

Kingston has made the experience of war a central focus of her literary career. (Deborah Madsen, *Maxine Hong Kingston*, p. 14)

This chapter examines Maxine Hong Kingston's latest novel, *The Fifth Book of Peace* (2003), and suggests that in addition to her popularity as a feminist writer, she deserves recognition as a pacifist writer and activist, and that we need to reconceive of her work as part of an on-going pacifist project. I make the claim that Kingston can be considered alongside other Asian American authors, notably Le-Ly Hayslip, as contributing towards the evolution of an Asian American women's peace literature.

Kingston as poet and peacemaker

'I have almost finished my longbook,' says Maxine Hong Kingston in *To Be the Poet* (2002). 'Let my life as a poet begin ... I have labored for over twelve years, one thousand pages of prose. Now I want the easiness of poetry ... I won't be a work-horse anymore; I'll be a skylark'.[1] *To Be the Poet* is a slim volume of meditation upon Kingston's life and work, past and future as a writer. It is based upon the William E. Massey Sr. Lectures in the History of American Civilization, given by Kingston at

Harvard University in 2000. It precedes, in both chronology of publication and subject matter, her long-awaited new novel, *The Fifth Book of Peace*, which was published in September 2003, and which replaced the manuscript of *Another Book of Peace* (she alternatively named it *The Book of Peace* and *The Fourth Book of Peace*), the book Kingston had nearly completed when her house burnt down in the 1991 Oakland, California fires. Given the labour involved in recreating her novel, it is not surprising that Kingston wanted to pause to draw breath and reflect upon her achievements and aspirations as a writer at this point in her life. *To Be the Poet* reads like an interregnum. Here Kingston allows herself the luxury of extensive reflection upon poetic and other creative practice, including the politics of form, the discipline required to write, the teaching and sharing of poetry, and theories of writing poetry. Although Kingston has periodically mused at some length upon the process and practice of writing – there are countless interviews with her published, as the selected bibliography attests – this book provides a neat collection of her philosophy, not just of poetry, but of life and living, importantly including her pacifist and eco-feminist politics, her attitude to ageing (she recently turned sixty), and her enjoyment of mothering, all of which are recurrent preoccupations of *The Fifth Book of Peace* as well. What comes across is Kingston's clear enjoyment of her life, and her security of self.

To Be the Poet is split into three sections: 'I Choose the Poet's Life', 'I Call on the Muses of Poetry, and Here's What I Get', and 'Spring Harvest'. The first section is full of optimism and enthusiasm, and Kingston is eager to embark upon a new phase of her life following the completion of her novel. The second, as its title suggests, is less whimsical and more humorous, in which Kingston dismantles the processes of writing, and records her life between March and April, 2000, during the writing of *The Fifth Book of Peace*. The final section interweaves poetry and prose reflection, and as Kingston notes, ends her 'season of poetry' (*TBP*, p. 111). All these sections include Kingston's own sketchings, which are interspersed with various recollections and poems. Taken as a whole, the book offers a fascinating glimpse into this writer's life, as well as offering what comes close to a manifesto of Kingston's praxis as a pacifist artist.

In a 2004 interview with me, Kingston remarked, 'Looking over all my books, you can see a war in the background of each one. I was born into WWII, and immediately thought about what a single individual could do to stop it. When I came to know history, I wrote about wars long ago – the War of the Three Kingdoms, the American Civil War, etc. And always: Where is the happy ending?' Here, as in *The Fifth Book of Peace*, Kingston brings her desire to shape fiction from life to bear upon her interrogation of the (il)logic of war. For her, if the impetus of her political agenda is pacifism, then as a writer she seeks to craft an orderly – logical – narrative from the stuff of history. And yet the abiding lesson of this latest novel is the inevitable failure of such a project. The penultimate section of *The Fifth Book of Peace* opens with this conclusion:

> I wrote past the place where the burned book left off. But found no happy ending. The war in Viet Nam won't come to a happy ending. Fiction won't tell me … Things that fiction can't solve must be worked out in life.[2]

In drawing attention to the messiness of the Vietnam War – its lack of a neat ending – Kingston is following a by-now established and widely acknowledged scholarly view.[3] For instance, in *Vietnam: Anatomy of a Peace*, Gabriel Kolko writes:

> All wars profoundly transmute social and human realities, and it is only with this pervasive truth in mind that we can begin to comprehend the whole course of Vietnam's history, not only over the thirty years of the war but, above all, after it ended in 1975. There is a direct continuity between the war's overwhelming heritage and the two decades that followed it. We cannot understand the anatomy of the peace unless we fully appreciate the war's incalculable physical, human, and psychological damage.[4]

At one point in Kingston's novel, the central male protagonist, Wittman, observes that 'Sanctuary was not just theater – it was school'. For Kingston, *The Fifth Book of Peace* is not just fiction, it is a manifesto. What, then, is she trying to achieve?

Hawai'ian peace

Kingston has a very clear sense of her mandate in *The Fifth Book of Peace*. 'If I could strongly write peace, I can cause an end to war,' she said in 1993.[5] This is echoed in her call – not to arms, but to peace, at the end of the novel:

> Children, everybody, here's what to do during war: In a time of destruction, create something. A poem. A parade. A community. A school. A vow. A moral principle. One peaceful moment. (*FBP*, p. 402)

In one Vietnam veteran's words, 'You want to hear a gen-u-ine war story? I only understand Vietnam as though it were a story.'[6] As the forgoing quotation attests, Kingston's initial motivation for writing *The Fifth Book of Peace* was precisely to narrativise the Vietnam War and make the case for an on-going peace. She has always adopted the perspective of the so-called 'dove critique' to the war in Vietnam. This view, popularised by the sixties' anti-war movement, recognised the illegitimacy and corruption of Diem's South Vietnamese government, and even acknowledged the strategic importance of Vietnam in the cold war political landscape of Southeast Asia, but nevertheless insisted upon the fundamental immorality and brutality of a war which made such extensive use of toxic defoliants and napalm, and which involved the bombing and burning of villages, the torture of innocent civilians and the widespread destruction of an entire environment.

In *The Fifth Book of Peace* Kingston takes her inspiration for, and versions of, peace from many sources. One source is Hawai'i, where a portion of the novel is set. In a 2004 interview with me, Kingston observed: 'The Hawai'ian culture has many concepts for making peace. The world knows about *aloha*. I want to spread the idea of *ohana* as well – the Beloved Community, according to Martin Luther King Jr. And *ho'oponopono* – gathering and talking out difficulties' (italics mine). In *The Fifth Book of Peace*, Kingston expands upon the definition: '"ho'oponopono" … means "to put to rights,"' she tells us,

> To this day people in Hawai'i have ho'ponopono, a
> conference where they talk and listen, explain, pray,
> confess, apologize, and at last understand and forgive and
> reconcile everything and everyone. Ho'oponopono makes
> aloha possible. (*FBP*, p. 204)

In *The Fifth Book of Peace* Kingston connects her promotion of
the practice of *ho'oponopono* with her articulation of Buddhist
philosophy, which has become increasingly important to her in
latter years. In particular, she evokes the Buddhist concept of
sangha. As she describes it in the novel, this is

> The Buddhist word for the community that lives in peace
> and harmony. ... To live happily, wholly, truly, each of us
> has to create sangha. The sangha is the place – the sangha
> is the people with whom you can exchange feelings and
> thoughts. The sangha inspires you, and keeps you thriv-
> ing, and makes life worth living. Build the community
> with resources at hand, whatever's, whoever's here, whoever
> shows up, whoever happens by. Make community, *com-
> munitas*, sangha of those people in your apartment
> building, on your street, at your job, wherever you are.
> (*FBP*, p. 364)

Throughout *The Fifth Book of Peace*, the stories and anecdotes
of war – and war protest – as told by Kingston, veterans and
others, when filtered through the lens of *sangha*, become a literature of peace, which ultimately comes to affirm, for Kingston
and for her readers, the transformative power of fiction; as she
says: 'War causes peace' (*FBP*, p. 227).

Kingston's interest in Buddhism is central to *The Fifth Book
of Peace*, although it can actually be traced back to her early
writing years. In 1980, while she was still living in Hawai'i, she
was even named a 'Living Treasure of Hawaii' by a Honolulu
Buddhist sect. Stemming from Zen logic, Buddhism promotes
the concept of 'nonattachment' to all things (including invidious
ideologies), and so is in fundamental conflict with the Cold War
ideologies which prevailed during Kingston's adolescence. This
concept of 'nonattachment' is also connected to the concept of
'compassion', as well as non-violence (and here Buddhism over-

laps with a Hindhu-inspired form of pacifism espoused by Mohandas Karamchand Gandhi as *satyagraha*, and, later, Martin Luther King's Christian reformation of non-violence). Kingston's interest in these forms of pacifism and peaceful protest actually stretches back to her involvement in student anti-war protests in the highly politicised milieu of Berkeley in the 1960s, where she was a student between 1958 and 1962, and it is a period she recalls with some nostalgia. She was living in Berkeley in 1961, though, when President John F. Kennedy ordered soldiers to Vietnam, and later, when, in 1965, President Lyndon Johnson escalated the war in Vietnam, and Berkeley students responded with 'teach-ins' on campus.[7] More recently, her involvement in pacifism saw her attend a conference in San Francisco in 1997, called 'Peacemaking: The Power of Nonviolence', and in the Epilogue to *The Fifth Book of Peace*, Kingston recounts her participation in the peace protests against war in Iraq on International Women's Day, 2002. Several set-pieces from Kingston's early writing also mark her long-standing concern with pacifism, including 'War' in *Hawai'i One Summer*, and the section 'The Brother in Vietnam' in *China Men*. And finally we can observe an awareness of American domestic opposition to the military conflict in Southeast Asia, which is an abiding backdrop to all of Kingston's writing, as she remarks:

> The whole question of war and peace begins in *The Woman Warrior* ... That little child is really worried. There's bombs going off. What war is this? How come is this called World War Two? Was there a One? Will there be a Three? What's going on here? And I write about the trauma of seeing my first movie, which was a war movie. I'm wasting all my wishes on war. And so I see that I have had the same concerns from the very start and I'm bringing them more and more into mature thinking.[8]

The Fifth Book of Peace has four sections: 'Fire', 'Paper', 'Water' and 'Earth'. Although these are not strictly elements, each section corresponds to an 'elemental' preoccupation in the text, as Kingston remarks elsewhere in the book: 'Searching for books has led me to bones, water, clouds, choreography' (*FBP*, p. 55), and they relate to the predominant 'texture' of each section. 'Fire' opens with the Oakland Fires of 1992; 'Paper' describes Kingston's search for the textual – paper – traces of the mythical Books of Peace; 'Water' takes us to the Hawai'ian Islands and the final section, 'Earth', returns us to the Berkeley of the later 1990s and Kingston's literal and metaphorical rebuilding of her life from the ashes of the fire. If this seems a rather complicated and schematic narrative structure, then this simply reflects Kingston's desire to incorporate the process of reconstructing her lost novel, as well as the actual novel itself. In 1993, she described how

> this new book is going to be very complicated. I've decided to leave in all the stuff about how to get into the thinking mind, the mind that can write. How do you get into words again? I am going to leave all that in. That's about a third of the book. Next I get into the book that I was writing, which is the fiction about Wittman. Then finally I come out of the fiction. So this book enters a real nonfiction place, then it flies to a fiction place, and then it grounds us again in a nonfiction place. I haven't seen another book like it, nor, once again, do I know how people will categorize it. Are they going to call it fiction or nonfiction? It is a nonfiction fiction nonfiction sandwich.[9]

In fact, the text is able to move quite easily between fiction and nonfiction modes. Kingston is a past master at combining generic registers, and could even be said to have built her literary reputation upon the (con)fusion of fictional and life-writing modes in her earlier works *The Woman Warrior* and *China Men*, as she does again here. In *Three Guineas* Virginia Woolf suggested that women could best write (about) peace 'by not repeating your words and following your methods but by finding new words and creating new methods'.[10] Peggy Kamuf notes that Woolf achieved this through making 'the borderline between fiction and history fluid', so perhaps there are also precedents for Kingston's own mixed-genre mode of pacifist inscription.[11]

'Fire'

The first section of the novel, 'Fire', opens with Kingston driving home from her father's funeral in 1992 to find the entire hills of Berkeley in flames. In a first-person, dramatic reconstruction of her attempt to locate her house, and recover the manuscript of *Another Book of Peace*, Kingston describes what CNN would later refer to as a 'picturesque burnscape' (*FBP*, p. 12). The fires occurred co-terminously with the first Gulf War, and Kingston's narrative is heavily imbued with her simultaneous horror at the War, and her disquiet at the bizarre coincidence of the fires starting at the same time:

> I know why this fire. God is showing us Iraq. It is wrong to kill, and refuse to look at what we've done. (*FBP*, p. 13)

Kingston concludes that she must learn to rationalise her personal loss – of book, home and possessions – as a kind of 'shadow experience' of the war. This opening 'burnscape sequence' then propels us – and Kingston – into the main project, which is three fold: to reconstruct her novel, to rebuild her life and home, and to help the veterans of war, past and present, locate peace. Each strand of Kingston's endeavour, then, which was to preoccupy her for the entire 1990s (as *To Be the Poet* attests), braids together to form an all-consuming, multi-faceted, search and struggle for peace.

Shortly after the fire, Kingston attends a dream conference in Salado, Texas, where she asks the assembled dream experts to help her to find her lost book: 'Please send me anything you find about lost Books of Peace, cities of refuge, tactics for stopping war' (*FBP*, p. 42) she pleads. In the immediate aftermath of the loss of her work, a shocked Kingston found that she had lost the ability to write: 'I could not re-enter fiction' (*FBP*, p. 61).[12] The conference proves cathartic though, and by the end of this section, Kingston is able to talk of a 'book-to-be' (*FBP*, p. 42), and she begins her search for the lost books of peace, which is the pre-occupation of the next section. This search leads to proliferating possibilities as the so-called 'books of peace' seem to exist in many times and places.

'Paper' and 'Water'

'Paper' opens with the comment that 'Supposedly, a long time ago in China, there existed Books of Peace' (*FBP*, p. 45). The original Chinese books of peace, we are told, were 'lost in deliberate fires' (and here we find intentional echoes of the author's own plight). In 1991 Kingston told interviewer Donna Perry:

> The Chinese have this tradition, that once upon a time there were these three books of peace that had all kinds of directions on how to have non-violent communication. The myth is that these books were burned, and so we don't know what was in them – we don't know their effects. So I think of it as, that's what I have to do. I have to rewrite them, to try and figure out what was in them, to bring them back.[13]

Other possible books of peace were found on the Silk Road in Western China, in the eleventh century, or were actually 'oracle bones' – with hexagrams of war and peace carved upon them. The peace hexagram, 'T'ai' offers another hope, as does 'The Book of Songs. The Book of History. The Book of Rites. The Spring and Autumn Annals. Confucius. Lao Tzu. Mo Tzu. Mencius on social utopias' (*FBP*, p. 48), The Art of War by Sun Tzu and *Heart Sutra* from India. But, 'The Fourth Book of Peace … was fiction', we are told,

> It had to be fiction, because Peace has to be supposed, imagined, divined, dreamed. Peace's language, its sounds and rhythms, when read aloud, when read silently, should pacify breath and tongue, make ears and brain be tranquil. (*FBP*, p. 61)

Armed, as it were, with the conviction that she must reconstruct the narratives of peace, Kingston realises her path towards recreating her novel lies in her own past: 'I should be able to write again about the time Earll and I took our son, Joseph, and left to live in Hawai'i' (*FBP*, p. 61).

The third, and longest, section of the book, 'Water', returns us, then, to familiar Kingston territory. Here, Kingston imaginatively reconstructs her lost novel, which reunites us with Wittman Ah Sing and his wife Taña, the protagonists of Kingston's 1989 novel about sixties hippie culture, *Tripmaster Monkey: His Fake Book*. It is still the sixties, and, following the route taken by Kingston and her husband, Wittman and Taña and their son Mario are heading for Hawai'i in order to evade the draft. Refiguring these familiar characters from her earlier work as peace activists in *The Fifth Book of Peace* enables Kingston to simultaneously key into the countercultural vein of *Tripmaster* and to stage the debates for and against American involvement in Vietnam. Kingston builds upon Wittman's *Tripmaster* identity as a beatnik and graduate of Berkeley, and Taña's as his persistent hippie companion and, later, wife in the alternative religion of the Universal Life Church. However, although Wittman and Taña seek to escape the war, they actually find that, paradoxically, in some ways they move closer to it, since the Hawai'i they move to turns out to be s highly militarised environment, and the islands are also full of Vietnam soldiers who have gone AWOL. In a sense this reflects the Kingstons' own experiences when they too tried to distance themselves physically – and culturally – from the war by moving to the islands. This, in fact, may have instigated, or at least strengthened, Kingston's pacifism in earlier years. She has remarked that 'Anti-draft work intrudes on my life, so I just put my resentment right back into the struggle'.[14] It is worth noting, though, that Kingston's *Tripmaster* characters, Wittman and Taña, actually became involved in anti-war protest even in her earlier novel. It was the draft that initiated their marriage for instance (since at that time, married men were exempt from conscription), and many of the war debates of *The Fifth Book of Peace*, including the legitimacy of the lottery of conscription, are rehearsed in *Tripmaster Monkey* as well. In her 1993 interview with Neila C. Seshachari, aptly entitled, 'Reinventing Peace', Kingston explains the relationship between the two books:

> *Tripmaster Monkey* ends during Wittman's late adolescence. Wittman is a boyish person and he has just gotten married but there's no commitment of understanding of

what marriage is. Not enough time has gone by to test the marriage, to test the carrying out of one's values and principles. The story ends when he decides that he will be a draft evader. You know, for young people there are these instant decisions. But the real test of a human being is a long term carrying out of ideas, and so the next book is about Wittman becoming older and middle aged.[15]

Kingston figures Wittman's maturation as filtered, then, through his gradual commitment to a pacifist politics. Once they have settled in Kahalu'u, Wittman and Tana become involved in the pacifist protests occurring across the islands, which for the protesters often involves an accompanying exploration of various historical theories of peace, and an analysis of their practitioners: 'Jesus and Gandhi and Martin Luther King, Jr., taught us to be peaceful, silent, loving in response to ignorance and anger', Kingston observes (*FBP*, p. 131). The protesters decide to create a sanctuary for deserters. Spelt with a capital, 'Sanctuary' is not merely a physical refuge in the novel, but instead becomes the physical embodiment of a literal and spiritual life-choice, as Wittman explains: 'Sanctuary is a place of safety in the midst of a society at war' (*FBP*, p. 195), and later, in a description which seems to ventriloquise Kingston: 'Above all laws, it is the duty to stop or destroy any force which interferes with positive human life forces' (*FBP*, p. 196). In fact, the concept of 'sanctuary' has many applications in *The Fifth Book of Peace*, here in the section 'Water' and elsewhere, as a personal as well as political space, physical and metaphorical sanctuary, home for the veterans and too for Kingston herself. The 'Sanctuary' in *The Fifth Book of Peace* is also another of the many autobiographical parallels we find between Kingston's fiction and her own life, since it is actually based upon a real Sanctuary, at the Church of the Crossroads, in Hawai'i, where Kingston remembers 'the AWOL soldiers who were true pacifist heroes' (*HOS*, p. xv).

'Earth'

The fourth section, 'Earth', takes us back to Berkeley in the present day, and to Kingston's relationship with her mother, the indomitable figure of Brave Orchid who featured prominently in *The Woman Warrior*, and picks up once more the author's efforts to repair her life in post-fire Oakland. In a predictable manner, and one which is very reminiscent of *The Woman Warrior*, it is Brave Orchid who shakes her daughter out of her post-fire stasis, and spurs her on to her next project:

> My mother comes to me in dreams. She is at her largest and most powerful, midlife. My age now. She says, 'What have you been doing to educate America? What have you done to educate the world? Have you taught everybody yet?' The Chinese idiom for 'everybody' is 'big family'. (*FBP*, p. 241)

As she has always done, Kingston takes up her mother's challenge. Her aim is to help to heal the veterans of war, who, in answer to her earlier call for books of peace, have begun to send her the stories of war:

> How should I reply to these people? In person. I have to look in their eyes and faces, and tell them, You are home. Thankyou. I have to give them something, reciprocate gifts. And happy-end the wars. (*FBP*, p. 248)

Kingston achieves this by holding a series of healing, writing workshops for veterans of Vietnam across the country (which she also documents at length in *To Be the Poet*). Once more, her response is to craft stories: 'What to do in war's aftermath? Make a story. Tell the story until a happy ending' (*FBP*, p. 329). She incorporates the very stories and reminiscences related to her by the veterans as part of her own narrative, some of which are extremely harrowing. It is as if the author cannot herself speak these horrors, but must allow them to be told by others, and in fact at certain points in the wake of horrific tales, Kingston seems to be almost silenced by the stories.

This process of healing and reconstruction culminates in a visit to the Buddhist monk and teacher, Thich Nhat Hanh's spiritual community, Plum Village, in rural France. Thich Nhat Hanh is an important Buddhist teacher and veteran of the Buddhist peace movement in Vietnam. Buddhist monks were involved in some of the most extreme – and effective – protests against the anti-Buddhist policies of the South Vietnamese president Ngo Dinh Diem in the early 1960s. Many monks, and most infamously, Buddhist monk Quang Duc, immolated them-selves in public places in Saigon, the pictures of which were swiftly syndicated world-wide, and helped to attract international attention to the conflict. Eventually, Buddhist opposition to the Catholic-dominant Saigon regime culminated in the expulsion of large numbers of Vietnamese Buddhist monks, Thich Nhat Hanh included, and he now resides in exile in France. Thich Nhat Hanh's role in the opposition to war in Vietnam was a pivotal one. Here it is described by Robert J. Topmiller in his book, *The Lotus Unleashed: The Buddhist Peace Movement in South Vietnam, 1964–1966*:

> Some Buddhists perceived the deep distress in South Viet-namese society over the war and responded with calls for peace. Sensing significant war-weariness after a quarter-century of conflict, Thich Nhat Hanh introduced a resolu-tion calling for an end to the fighting during a conference of monks early in 1964. A diminutive, gentle-looking monk who radiated serenity and compassion, he eventually became an eloquent spokesman for peace in Vietnam by focusing on the moral malaise that had descended on the country as a result of the rapid changes brought on by the conflict. He also helped reintroduce the concept of Engaged Buddhism, a militant social activism that ignored both sides of the hostilities and concentrated on bringing succour to its victims.[16]

Thich Nhat Hanh has become an important spiritual influence upon Kingston, and has introduced her to his Buddhist teach-ings. Several years ago, Kingston attended one of his retreats, called 'Healing the Wounds of War', and it was as a result of this that Kingston decided to become involved with Vietnam veterans who comprised, and continue to comprise, many of Thich Nhat Hanh's students. At the time, Kingston felt strongly that while Thich Nhat Hanh was able to provide a spiritual form of healing for his veteran students, the retreats lacked an artistic dimension. This she was able to provide, and many years ago, she became involved in offering writing workshops during the Buddhist retreat. Eventually, as a result of a Lila Wallace Fund Fellowship in 1992, Kingston was able to expand upon this work and to hold writing workshops specifically for Vietnam veterans, and thus to create writing communities for veterans – of war and peace. At the end of *The Fifth Book of Peace* Kingston accompanies a group of veterans on a quasi-pilgrimage, which is filmed by the BBC for a series entitled 'Stories My Country Told Me'. In a series of vignette-like sequences, Kingston expresses her pleasure at witnessing the peace and *sangha* experienced by the veterans. In her interview, 'Reinventing Peace' (1993), Kingston told Neila Seshachari:

> The end to the Vietnam War is not just that they stop shooting and we stop shooting. That's not the end. The end has to be something very wonderful. The Vietnamese have a commune in France. Thich Nhat Hanh, a Vietnamese monk, has a religious commune in France, and I was thinking how wonderful if I could bring a group of Vietnam veterans to live in community with Vietnamese people. ... To me, that would be a true ending to the war with Vietnam.[17]

By taking up her mother's challenge to educate the world, and inheriting the mantle of peace, Kingston figures herself in this novel as something of a soothsayer, or prophet. Just as in the opening lines she declares that 'it is given her to know devastation' (*FBP*, p. 1), so she closes with a declaration of triumph over adversity: 'In writing this Book of Peace ... I had been able to tell Mother that I built a Sangha' (*FBP*, p. 297).

At the end of *The Fifth Book of Peace*, too, Kingston returns to her story of Fa Mu Lan (rendered here as 'Fa Mook Lan'), which was so central in *The Woman Warrior* in providing an inspirational metaphor of combative, assertive womanhood. Inspirational here too, Kingston recycles it as a peace story, of homecoming:

> I chanted my Woman Warrior Chant. I learned it from my mother, and now tried to translate it as closely as possible. It is about a Mook Lan, who disguised herself as a man and fought a war against the Tatars. I have told it as a woman's liberation story, and as a war story. But now I understand it, it is a homecoming story. Fa Mook Lan leads her army home from war. She shows the troops herself changing back from a man to a woman, and gives them a vision of the feminine. Veterans can return to civil society. They do not have to be homeless. (*FBP*, p. 390)

'Jik jik jik' or 'weave weave weave' is the chant she uses, as Fa Mook Lan was also a weaver. In emphasising this, Kingston reclaims the power of her woman warrior: no longer does this rest upon her combative abilities, rather Fa Mook Lan's strength is now seen to lie in her creativity. Kingston has often expressed her regret at figuring female resilience through war imagery in *The Woman Warrior*; here, then, she is able to correct this.

Towards an Asian American women's peace canon: Kingston and Le Ly Hayslip

The multi-genre peace story that Kingston has crafted in *The Fifth Book of Peace* forms an interesting intertextual relationship with other forms of Vietnam literature. Specifically from a pacifist perspective, two important co-texts to *The Fifth Book of Peace* are the autobiographical novels by Vietnamese American woman writer Le Ly Hayslip, entitled *When Heaven and Earth Changed Places* (1989) and *Child of War, Woman of Peace* (1993). Le Ly Hayslip's two-book life-writing project mirrors Kingston's own work in many ways, not least in her own vexed relationship with the conflict in Vietnam as an Asian American woman. Like Kingston, Hayslip spent many years outside of the US (for Hayslip, in Vietnam) which provided her with a differently nuanced perspective on the Vietnam conflict. Hers is a position of insider–outsider: she was actively involved in the conflict, as a peasant imprisoned and then tortured and raped by the ARVN (the army of South Vietnam), before her eventual escape from the country via Da Nang and Saigon in 1973. *When Heaven and Earth Changed Places* is her account (mediated via the writer Jay Wurts) of this experience. Her subsequent life in the US, married to an American civilian, coupled with frequent visits to Vietnam forms the subject of the companion text, *Child of War, Woman of Peace* (co-written with her son James). This text is important for our purposes, because of its documentary of Hayslip's increasing involvement with healing the wounds of Vietnam in a post-conflict era, which was especially concentrated upon the survivors of the war, both American and Vietnamese, and also for what has been termed Hayslip's 'gendered pacifism'.[18] In a narrative conclusion which echoes the end of Kingston's story, *Child of War, Woman of Peace* culminates in Hayslip's return to Vietnam to build a health clinic and reconcile with her family. Like Kingston's narrative, too, Hayslip's text pays much attention to the process and pain of writing a war story.

In addition to these similarities, Hayslip's memoirs provide a useful counterpoint to *The Fifth Book of Peace* since despite the status of both authors as 'Asian American', each narrative emerges from a very different perspective upon the conflict and each author had markedly different degrees of involvement in the conflict itself. Hayslip's voice is one of a very few telling not only the Vietnamese story of war and its aftermath through the medium of English, but is also one of only a few narratives from a female perspective as well. The implications of this are manifold, and inevitably include a degree of mediation in each text; a discernible tendency to oscillate between alliance with different sides in the conflict; an advocacy of reconciliation; and ultimately a refusal to apportion blame to any one side.

The gender implications of Hayslip's different positioning are, if anything, even more complex. Angela K. Smith says of women who have engaged in conflict:

For women it is different. To participate in war, on many
levels, they need to break traditional codes of femininity.
Even as victims and casualties they trespass into a male
arena.[19]

As critics such as Angela K. Smith have shown, male-authored
representations of the Vietnam conflict and its consequences have
been hampered by stereotypes of suffering veterans and of 'graphic-
ally violent representation',[20] whereas in Hayslip's writing, there
is an attempt to move beyond this, to explore the effects of the
conflict upon family and community dynamics, damage wreaked
on an individual, psychological level, and an attempt to unpick
an aggressor/victim binary, by figuring *all* those involved in the
conflict as victims. In *The Writing of War*, William Cloonan
observes that women writers have tended to avoid extended narratives of conflict, and choose instead to write of war's consequences, as both Kingston and Hayslip here, opt to do too.[21] In
Hayslip's work there is also an extensive meditation upon the
connected issues of violence and healing, and a heavy emphasis
upon Buddhist spirituality. Here then, Hayslip comes close to
the exploration of war and its consequences we find in *The Fifth
Book of Peace*, in which Kingston's 'gendered pacifism' can be seen
to mirror Hayslip's. Via this, as William Cloonan observes (p. 76),
warfare simply 'becomes another form of patriarchal oppression'.

A further, even more immediate connection between the
two authors can be found in the opening pages of *When Heaven
and Earth Changed Places*, where we find reference to a 'woman
warrior', intended no doubt as an explicit reference to Kingston's
first work, *The Woman Warrior*, published some years earlier,
and, at the time when Hayslip was writing, already in its heyday
of popularity. The textual impetus of Hayslip's work is to move
from war chronicler, and the figure of the woman warrior, to a
meditation upon peace; or from 'child of war' to 'woman of
peace' to echo her own title, as it was too for Kingston, who, like
Hayslip, found it necessary to reformulate her notion of 'woman
in combat' to 'woman at – and in – peace'. Taken together, then,
the works of Hayslip and Kingston may constitute the beginnings of a corpus of a new literature – a literature of peace.

Critical overview

Asian American literature by women is increasingly attracting critical attention as an important sub genre of American literature. Current debates over the literary canon, the changing profile of literary and cultural studies, the increasing presence of women's and ethnic writing both within and beyond the canon may all explain the increasing popularity of Asian American women's writing both within the US and beyond its geographical borders. Yet, the critical debate on Asian American women's writing has barely begun when compared with resources available for readers of African American, say, or Native American writing. In the context of the canon of Asian American writing by women, the publication of *The Woman Warrior*, in 1976, precipitated an intense period of growth, and *The Woman Warrior* swiftly became the first classic of Asian American literature. Since that time, something of a revolution has occurred in the development and visibility of both ethnic writing by women generally (the popularity of the African American writers Alice Walker and Toni Morrison are such examples), and the specific expansion of writing in print by Asian American women, by authors like Bharati Mukherjee, Nora Okja Keller, Lois-Ann Yamanaka, Ginu Kamani, Ruth Ozeki and Wendy Law-Yone. The works of Amy Tan, Jung Chang, Anchee Min and Adeline Yen Mah, for example, have built upon and consolidated the emergence of Asian American and Asian British writing as particular corpuses; all of which have achieved high sales figures and wide media interest. It is clear, therefore, that in the period since 1976 there has been a distinct emerging canon of Asian American women's writing, which coincides with the surge in popularity of ethnic women's writing in recent decades.

There has thus been a consistent scholarly interest in Maxine Hong Kingston's work, but this has tended to concentrate upon her now-notorious feud with fellow Chinese American writer, Frank Chin (eg Wong 1992), or has explored the vexed issue of *The Woman Warrior*'s generic status (eg Lidoff 1987; Smith 1987), or has included Kingston in delineations of the development of Asian American literature (eg Lim and Ling 1992; Cheung 1997), or Asian American women's writing (Ling 1990; Cheung 1993; Bow 2001; Grice 2002; Chiu 2004; Duncan 2004).[1] Book-length critical works on Kingston (all published in the United States) include two books of critical essays (Skandera-Trombley 1998; Wong 1999), an edited collection of essays (Skenazy and Martin 1998), a pedagogically oriented edited collection (Lim 1991) and three survey works (Madsen 2000; Huntley 2001; Crow 2004). Specific studies also exist on aspects of Kingston's work: Gao (1996) explores Kingston's use of Chinese sources; Simmons (1999) reads Kingston's three major works from the period 1976–1989 in relation to the theme of transcendence; and Rusk (2002) analyses Kingston's 'life writing of otherness', in juxtaposition with other contemporary women writers like Jeanette Winterson. While this list attests to Kingston's status as a major literary figure, it also highlights the absence of an extensive study devoted to her entire oeuvre, which includes the major redirection her work has taken since 2002 towards an engagement with a politics of pacifism and eco-feminism (an omission this study seeks to partly redress). Recent studies look beyond the appeal of Maxine Hong Kingston's life writing, in order to both locate her work more thoroughly within a tradition of writing about twentieth-century China, and to pay attention to her political concerns and legacies, which have been made most manifest in her books published since 2002. For instance, Patti Duncan's *Tell This Silence: Asian American Women Writers and the Politics of Speech* (2004), argues that Kingston's writing constitutes an oppositional endeavour which works to resist official, exclusionary U.S. histories of Asian immigration.

Critical work on Kingston has been heavily dominated by a focus upon *The Woman Warrior*, and to a lesser degree, *China Men*. Early responses to *The Woman Warrior* in particular tended to focus upon Kingston's use of Chinese sources, and became very dominated by the controversies surrounding her work to which I allude above. An overview of this may be found in Sau-ling Wong's essay, 'Kingston's Handling of Traditional Chinese Sources' (1991), which defended Kingston's work from the *Aiiieeeee!* critics and others. Later criticism approached the narrative from a range of different contexts. Many analyses viewed the text as coinciding with a moment in feminist studies and feminist literary production when the mother/daughter dyad became a focus of particular interest. In *Between Worlds: Women Writers of Chinese Ancestry* (1990), Amy Ling reads *The Woman Warrior* alongside Amy Tan's work in order to explore the 'problematic Chinese mother–American daughter relationship' (p. 130). More recently, Wendy Ho's 1999 study, *In Her Mother's House: The Politics of Asian American Mother–Daughter Writing*, views Kingston's writing as an exploration of the ambivalence of the mother/daughter relationship, in which the daughter at once desires a separation from, but acknowledges a debt to, the mother figure as a source of subjectivity. Sheryl A. Mylan has read the text as demonstrating an intercultural orientalism in her interesting piece, 'The Mother as Other: Orientalism in Maxine Hong Kingston's *The Woman Warrior*' (1996). Other approaches have explored the silence–speech dichotomy at work in the text. An early journal article by Linda Morante, 'From Silence to Song: the Triumph of Maxine Hong Kingston' (1987), has been followed by several other analyses, including King-kok Cheung's book-length study, *Articulate Silences: Hisaye Yamamoto, Maxine Hong Kingston, Joy Kogawa* (1993), in which Cheung reads *The Woman Warrior* alongside work by other Asian American woman writers as manifesting a particular emphasis upon the importance of silence as a strategic weapon against oppression. In addition, attention has been paid to Kingston's mixture of generic modes in her life writing, and the text has been read as emblematic of a specifically female mode of auto/biographical writing. Sidonie Smith has explored the text from the perspective of filiality and women's autobiographical storytelling (1987); Leigh Gilmore has built upon this work in analysing Kingston's focus upon the body in her quest for self-representation (1994). Another strand of criticism has sought to locate the text within the development of ethnic women's writing, and Asian American writing in particular. One example is Mary Dearborn's *Pocahontas's Daughters: Gender and Ethnicity in American Culture* (1986). In another influential book, *All My Relatives: Community in Ethnic American Literatures* (1993), Bonnie TuSmith identifies a language of community to be found in texts like *The Woman Warrior*. Jeanne Rosier Smith has focused upon Kingston's use of trickster figures in her two life-writing texts, as a characteristic of ethnic women's writing in her study, *Writing Tricksters: Mythic Gambols in American Ethnic Literatures* (1997). In her book on Asian American writing, *Reading Asian American Literature: From Necessity to Extravagance* (1993), Sau-ling Wong approaches Kingston's work from the perspective of what she sees as a paradigmatic dichotomy in Asian American writing between the tropes of necessity and extravagance.

Auto/biographical and life-writing work are some of the most important ways in which Asian American women's voices from history can be recovered and heard. Auto/biographical expressions are also a means by which Asian American women are able to (re)claim a space for *self*-articulation and representation, against a history of external representation, stereotyping and partiality, which has characterised so much writing *about* Asian American women. Recent critical work on women's life-writing has both questioned inherited critical definitions of what constitutes life writing, and sought to enlarge the women's life-writing canon. Such studies have explored women's life writing as often fragmented, rather than chronologically developmental, in line with the fragmentary nature of both memory and self-hood; and texts such as Kingston's *The Woman Warrior* and

China Men have been examined for their episodic structure, and their tendency not to make observations or claims in the name of their wider societies. Interesting discussions of Kingston's two-book life-writing project have appeared in Sidonie Smith's *A Poetics of Women's Autobiography: Marginality and the Fictions of Self-Representation* (1987) and *Subjectivity, Identity, and the Body: Women's Autobiographical Practices in the Twentieth Century* (1993); and Françoise Lionnet's *Postcolonial Representations: Women, Literature, Identity* (1995).

Maxine Hong Kingston's contribution to Asian American feminism via her life writing is the subject of several other critical studies, such as Rachel Lee's discussion of Kingston in *The Americas of Asian American Literature: Gendered Fictions of Nation and Transnation* (1999); Leslie Bow's references to Kingston in *Betrayal and other Acts of Subversion: Feminism, Sexual Politics, Asian American Women's Literature* (2001); and as a more extended analysis in Sally Keenan's essay, 'Crossing Boundaries' (2000). This essay unusually not only focuses on *The Woman Warrior* but also on *China Men*, with some reference to *Tripmaster Monkey: His Fake Book*. The title of this essay, 'Crossing Boundaries', taken from a phrase in *The Woman Warrior* ('crossing boundaries not delineated in space'), is employed as a metaphor for two aspects of Kingston's work: its cultural politics, derived from her gendered cross-cultural identity, and its aesthetic practice, in particular the generic boundary crossings of her memoirs which are a mixture of autobiography and biography, history and myth, memory and fabulation. Keenan argues that such a mixture, although common in much postmodern writing, takes on a particular salience in Kingston's case since it provides her with a means to tease out the multiple threads of identity – of gender, ethnicity, class, culture and history. In this sense, Keenan argues that Kingston's writing occupies a seminal place in the recent history of feminist thought, in particular the watershed period of the late 1970s and early 1980s, and demonstrates how Kingston's work is symptomatic of a feminist understanding of all identities as mobile and continually open to renegotiation. This essay also

examines the ways in which Kingston's aesthetic practice drama-
tises a feminist understanding of the links between language and
identity: the acquisition of a mother tongue that is simultaneously her own and not her own, and through which the author
enacts a series of transcriptions or translations backwards and
forwards between Chinese and English idioms, creating in the
process a hybrid discourse embodying an Asian American
identity which also gives voice to a feminist consciousness.

Asian American feminist scholarship has been largely concerned with theorising the gender–ethnicity nexus; the structures
of Asian American women's multiple positionings: what Chicana
feminists have elsewhere named 'mestiza' consciousness; what
Sandra Kumamoto Stanley calls 'multiple consciousness'; or what
Amy Ling has named as 'outside the outside'; and 'between
worlds'. One of the most extensive essays to date which deals
with these issues is Shirley Geok-lin Lim's essay, 'Feminist and
Ethnic Literary Theories in Asian American Literature',
published in 1993. Lim argues for an 'ethnic-cultural nuancing
of conventional Euro-American feminist positions on gender/
power relations and a feminist critique of ethnic-specific identity'
(p. 572). Lim identifies the period of Asian American literary
production since the publication of Maxine Hong Kingston's
The Woman Warrior as exemplifying a 'conscious and explicit
conflict, between *women's* ideas of culture and cultural nationalism as claimed by some males' (p. 577). Arguing that the
catalyst for this split in Asian American literary studies was the
intervention of feminist critiques of literature and culture (with
accompanying foci upon the mother/daughter dyad and other
issues of gendered identity), Lim concludes that Asian American
women writers' complex negotiations of identity provide useful
paradigms of ethnic/gender identity which retain the sites of
conflict between differing ideological valuations of identity, and
refuse premature resolutions.

The gender/ethnicity problematic continues to remain a
vexed issue in Asian American feminist studies, and in particular most Asian American feminist discussions of Asian American
literature tend to address it to a greater or lesser extent. King-

kok Cheung's analysis of the modalities of silence in Asian American women's writing, in *Articulate Silences: Hisaye Yamamoto, Maxine Hong Kingston, Joy Kogawa* (1993), reads the work of these three Asian American women writers as manifesting a particular emphasis upon the importance of silence as a strategic weapon against oppression. Cheung furthermore argues that Anglo-American criticism of women's texts has tended to valorise speech at the expense of silence, and that this Eurocentric critical perception has obscured Asian American women writers' strategic deployment of a speech–silence dichotomy as both a countercultural tactic and as a means of dramatising the complexities and intersections of ethnicised and gendered identity.

Denationalisation is also a noticeable recent trend in Asian American feminist studies, as Sau-ling Wong has observed.[2] In using this term, Wong refers to three noticeable recent phenomena in Asian American studies: the 'easing of cultural nationalist concerns' (p. 1), academic cross-pollination between Asian American and Asian studies (what Wong calls the 'growing permeability between "Asian" and "Asian American"', p. 5), and the shift towards an increasingly globalised, or diasporic, perspective. The recent collaborative feminist work of Elaine Kim and Chungmoo Choi, the work of King-kok Cheung, and that of Lisa Lowe, are notable examples of this. Lisa Lowe's *Immigrant Acts: On Asian American Cultural Politics* (1996) uses feminist perspectives to analyse the position of Asian women in a global context, in relation to issues of colonialism, postcolonialism, nationalism, US interventions in Asian countries, the legacies of military dictatorships, and the ways in which these phenomena have affected Asian women in Asia, America and in the Asian diaspora. Against this, Kingston's work is identified as crystallising a conflict within Asian American discourse between a nationalist tug of allegiance and a globalist agenda. Laura Hyun Yi Kang's *Enfiguring Asian/American Women: Compositional Subjects* (2002), illustrates the manner in which writers like Kingston often become caught in the cross-sections of the meanings of 'Asian', 'American' and 'Women'.

If Sau-ling Wong is correct in her assertion that cultural nationalist concerns have 'eased' in recent years, then this is probably due to feminist critiques of Asian American cultural nationalist agendas.[3] King-kok Cheung's twin essays on this subject, *'The Woman Warrior* versus the Chinaman Pacific: Must a Chinese American Critic Choose between Feminism and Heroism?'* (1990), and her 1998 essay, 'Of Men and Men: Reconstructing Chinese American Masculinity', explore issues of gender politics in Asian American literature, with substantial reference to Kingston. Cheung argues that the representation of Asian men as 'emasculated' reflects the inextricability of gender and ethnic identity. She suggests that in response to this dominant representation, several Asian American male writers and critics have attempted to reconstruct Asian American masculinity by foregrounding and turning to Asian heroic traditions, such as martial arts, a move which has troubled Asian American feminists, leading to a conflict between Asian American feminists anxious to combat Asian American patriarchy and Asian American nationalists who have attacked what they view as Asian American feminists' reinforcement and perpetuation of negative stereotypes of Asian American men. In her attempt to reconfigure Asian American feminism, but at the same time anxious not to blunt Asian American male dissidence, Cheung explores possible avenues of reconciliation between Asian American feminist and nationalist agendas.

Notes

Chapter 1

1 Marilyn Chin (1989), 'Writing the Other: A Conversation with Maxine Hong Kingston', in Paul Skenazy and Tera Martin (eds), *Conversations with Maxine Hong Kingston* edited by (Jackson: University Press of Mississippi, 1998), pp. 86–104; p. 98.

2 Shelley Fisher Fishkin, 'Interview with Maxine Hong Kingston', in *Conversations with Maxine Hong Kingston*, as above, pp. 159–167; p. 167.

3 Amy Ling, *Between Worlds: Women Writers of Chinese Ancestry* (New York: Pergamon, 1990), p. 230. Also see Amy Ling, 'Chinese American Women Writers: The Tradition Behind Maxine Hong Kingston', in A. LaVonne Brown Ruoff and Jerry W. Ward, Jr. (eds), *Redefining American Literary History*, edited by (New York: The Modern Language Association of America, 1990), pp. 219–236.

4 Wendy Ho, 'Swan-Feather Mothers and Coca-Cola Daughters: Teaching Amy Tan's *The Joy Luck Club*', in John R. Maitino and David R. Peck (eds), *Teaching American Ethnic Literatures: Nineteen Essays* (Albuquerque: University of New Mexico Press, 1996), pp. 327–345; p. 339.

5 Sau-ling Wong and Jeffery Santa-Ana, 'Gender and Sexuality in Asian American Literature', *Signs: Journal of Women in Culture and Society*, 25:1 (1999), pp. 171–226; p. 221. In actual fact, very recent critical work, both on Kingston or Tan specifically, and on Asian American women writers more generally, partly redresses this tendency. For instance, Patti Duncan's 2003 study, *Tell This Silence: Asian American Women Writers and the Politics of Speech* (Iowa City: University of Iowa Press, 2004), which explores speech and silence alongside definitions of women of colour and U.S. feminist movements, includes a lengthy discussion of Maxine

Hong Kingston, amongst other women writers, but Tan is absent from the discussion. In another case, Maureen Sabine's 2004 book, *Maxine Hong Kingston's Broken Book of Life: An Intertextual Study* (Honolulu: University of Hawai'i Press, 2004), which explores how the disproportionate strength of the feminist perspective in *The Woman Warrior* has obscured Kingston's other concerns, is actually at pains to assert the uniqueness of Kingston's writing, over and against other writers.

6   These terms are Sau-ling Wong's, in her extended discussion of the narrative mode of each book respectively. See her essay, 'Sugar Sisterhood', cited below (n. 12).

7   *Time* magazine rated *The Woman Warrior* as one of the top ten nonfiction works of the 1970s. David Leiwei Li notes that Kingston was the most prominent ethnic woman writer of the 1970s and 1980s, her popularity crucially predating that of both Alice Walker and Toni Morrison. See *Imagining the Nation: Asian American Literature and Cultural Consent* (Stanford: Stanford University Press, 1998), p. 57. *China Men* won the American Book Award and the National Book Award for nonfiction, and was nominated for the National Book Critics Circle Award and the Pulizer Prize.

8   'Gender and Sexuality in Asian American Literature', as above, p. 176.

9   It should also be remembered that while Kingston was writing *The Woman Warrior*, several key legislative changes also occurred which affected women. 1972 saw Congress approve the Equal Rights Amendment to the Constitution, and the introduction of affirmative action programmes in colleges and universities; and the landmark Supreme Court decision *Roe versus Wade* (1973) overruled state laws which prevented abortion in early pregnancy.

10 For example, Mitsuye Yamada's 1979 essay, 'Invisibility is an Un-natural Disaster: Reflections of an Asian American Woman', and her 1981 essay, 'Asian Pacific American Women and Feminism', critiqued the non-inclusion of Asian American women in feminist activist organisations. Both can be found in Cherrie Moraga and Gloria Anzaldúa (eds), *This Bridge Called My Back: Writings by Radical Women of Color* (New York: Kitchen Table, 1981).

11 Other ethnic feminist texts co-opted by the white feminist move-ment include Alice Walker's *The Color Purple* (1982), Gloria Anzaldúa's *Borderlands/La Frontera: The New Mestiza* (1987) and Sandra Cisneros's *The House on Mango Street* (1984).

12 Sau-ling C. Wong, 'Sugar Sisterhood: Situating the Amy Tan Phenomenon', in David Palumbo-Liu (ed.), *The Ethnic Canon:*

Histories, Institutions, and Interventions (Minneapolis: University of Minnesota Press, 1995), pp. 174–210; p. 177.

13 See Amy Ling, 'Chinese American Women Writers', as above, p. 136.

14 'Sugar Sisterhood', as above, p. 178.

15 Shirley Geok-lin Lim, 'Asian American Daughters Rewriting Asian Maternal Texts', in Shirley Hune et al. (eds), *Asian Americans: Comparative and Global Perspectives* (Pullman: Washington State University Press, 1991), pp. 239–248.

16 'Sugar Sisterhood', as above, p. 179.

17 Wendy Ho, *In Her Mother's House: The Politics of Asian American Mother–Daughter Writing* (New York: Altamira, 1999), p. 41.

18 Kingston has recalled how students on the Berkeley campus where she teaches have referred to *The Woman Warrior* in this way.

19 Rocío G. Davis, *Transcultural Reinventions: Asian American and Asian Canadian Short-Story Cycles* (Toronto: Tsar, 2001), p. 21.

20 Bonnie TuSmith, *All My Relatives: Community in Contemporary Ethnic American Literatures* (Ann Arbor: University of Michigan Press, 1993).

21 Ibid., pp. 5–15.

22 Leslie Bow, *Betrayal and other Acts of Subversion: Feminism, Sexual Politics, Asian American Women's Literature* (Princeton: Princeton University Press, 2001), p. 3; p. 72; p. 73.

23 Ibid., p. 71.

24 Ibid., p. 98.

25 Monica Chiu, *Filthy Fictions: Asian American Literature by Women* (New York: Altamira, 2004), p. 61.

26 In addition to Ginu Kamani's *Junglee Girl*, Chiu's contemporary examples include the work of Lois-Ann Yamanaka and Ruth Ozeki.

27 Ann Brooks, *Postfeminisms: Feminism, Cultural Theory and Cultural Forms* (New York: Routledge, 1997), pp. 1–2. Also see Caren Kaplan, Norma Alarcón and Minoo Moallem (eds), *Between Women and Nation: Nationalisms, Transnational Feminisms, and the State* (Durham: Duke University Press, 1999), especially Caren Kaplan and Inderpal Grewal's essay, 'Transnational Feminist Cultural Studies: Beyond the Marxism/Poststructuralism/Feminism Divides', pp. 349–364.

28 *Postfeminisms*, as above, p. 4.

29 Chela Sandoval, 'U.S. Third World Feminism: The Theory and

Method of Oppositional Consciousness', *Genders*, 10, pp. 1–24. Also see, Chela Sandoval, *Methodology of the Oppressed* (Minneapolis: University of Minnesota Press, 2000).

30   This is quoted in Anne Tyler's very interesting review of *China Men*, which was published in *The New Republic* on 21 June, 1980 (see the select bibliography).

31   'Writing the Other', as above, p. 94.

32   Maxine Hong Kingston, *The Woman Warrior* (London: Picador, 1976), p. 51.

33   Amy Tan's *The Joy Luck Club* also makes less explicit references to the cold war, noting the closure of China, which prohibited the exchange of information between family members in the text.

34   Karen Horton (1979), 'Honolulu Interview', in *Conversations with Maxine Hong Kingston*, as above, pp. 5–13; p. 8.

35   Like Tan, though, Kingston's China is largely imaginary, as she only visited China in 1984, several years after the completion of *The Woman Warrior* and *China Men*.

36   Neila C. Seshachari (1993), 'Reinventing Peace: Conversations with Tripmaster Maxine Hong Kingston', in *Conversations with Maxine Hong Kingston*, as above, pp. 192–214; p. 194.

37   Paul Skenazy (1989), 'Kingston at the University', in *Conversations with Maxine Hong Kingston*, as above, pp. 118–158; p. 139.

38   'Honolulu Interview', as above, p. 9.

39   Diane Simmons, *Maxine Hong Kingston* (New York: Twayne, 1999), p. 166.

40   'Kingston at the University', as above, p. 157.

41   *The Woman Warrior*, as above, p. 147.

42   Shirley Geok-lin Lim and Mayumi Tsutakawa (eds), *The Forbidden Stitch: An Asian American Women's Anthology* (Corvallis: Calyx, 1989), p. 12.

43   Phoebe Eng, *Warrior Lessons: An Asian American Woman's Journey into Power.* (New York: Pocket Books, 1999), p. 6.

Chapter 2

1   Gary Kubota (1977), 'Interview with Maxine Hong Kingston', in Paul Skenazy and Tera Martin (eds), *Conversations with Maxine*

Hong Kingston (Jackson: University Press of Mississippi, 1998), pp. 1–4; p. 3.

2 Maureen Sabine, *Maxine Hong Kingston's Broken Book of Life: An Intertextual Study of 'The Woman Warrior' and 'China Men'* (Honolulu: University of Hawai'i Press, 2004).

3 Sau-ling C. Wong, *Maxine Hong Kingston's* The Woman Warrior: *A Casebook* (New York: Oxford University Press, 1999), p. 3.

4 Anthony J. Fonseca, 'Maxine Hong Kingston', in Deborah L. Madsen (ed.), *Dictionary of Literary Biography: Asian American Writers* (Farmington Hills: Thompson Gale, 2005), pp. 163–180; p. 164.

5 Laura Hyun Yi Kang, *Compositional Subjects: Enfiguring Asian/American Women* (Durham: Duke University Press, 2002), p. 32.

6 Frank Chin, 'Letter to Maxine Hong Kingston', private correspondence.

7 Ben Tong, 'Critic of Admirer Sees Dumb Racist', *San Francisco Journal*, May 11th, 1977, p. 6.

8 Jeffery Paul Chan, 'The Mysterious West', *New York Review of Books*, April 28th, 1977, p. 41.

9 Katheryn M. Fong, 'An Open Letter/Review', *Bulletin for Concerned Asian Scholars*, 9:4 (1977), pp. 67–69; p. 67.

10 Karen Amano, 'An Interview with Maxine Hong Kingston', *Performing Arts*, 1994, pp. 9–12; pp. 8–9.

11 Kingston, Letter to Shawn Wong, November 3rd, 1976. 'Maxine Hong Kingston Papers', Bancroft Library, University of California, Berkeley.

12 Kingston, Letter to Shawn Wong, December, 1976, in Kingston papers, as above.

13 Throughout my discussion of *The Woman Warrior*, I use 'the young girl', 'the young Maxine', 'Maxine' and 'Kingston' interchangeably to refer to the life-writing persona in the text. I only use 'Kingston' in my references to the author.

14 Maxine Hong Kingston, *The Woman Warrior* (London: Picador, 1977), p. 11. All references are to this edition and hereafter are cited parenthetically in the text.

15 Sau-ling C. Wong, 'Kingston's Handling of Traditional Chinese Sources', in Shirley Geok-lin Lim (ed.), *Approaches to Teaching Maxine Hong Kingston's "The Woman Warrior"* (New York: MLA, 1991), pp. 26–36; p. 28.

16 Ibid.

17   Maxine Hong Kingston, 'Personal Statement', in *Approaches to Teaching Maxine Hong Kingston's* The Woman Warrior, as above, p. 24.

18   'Kingston's Handling of Traditional Chinese Sources', as above, p. 30.

19   Kingston, 'Personal Statement', as above, p. 24.

20   Barbara A. White, *Growing Up Female; Adolescent Girlhood in American Fiction* (Westport, Conn.: Greenwood Press, 1985), p. 3.

21   Ibid., p. 137; p. 139; p. 13.

22   Ibid., p. 141; p. 143; p. 156.

23   Ibid., p. 157.

24   Ibid., p. 159.

25   Ellen Morgan, 'The Feminist Novel of Androgynous Fantasy', *Frontiers* 11 (Fall, 1977), pp. 40–49; p. 41.

26   *Maxine Hong Kingston's Broken Book of Life*, as above, p. 17.

27   Ibid., p. 120.

28   *Growing Up Female*, as above, pp. 177–182.

29   *Maxine Hong Kingston's Broken Book of Life*, as above, p. 127.

30   *Growing Up Female*, pp. 147–148.

31   Jo Malin, *The Voice of the Mother: Embedded Maternal Narratives in Twentieth-Century Women's Autobiographies* (Carbondale and Edwardsville: Southern Illinois University Press, 2000), p. 1.

32   Ibid., p. 2.

33   Ibid., p. 6; p. 11.

34   Rita Felski, *Beyond Feminist Aesthetics* (Cambridge, MA: Harvard University Press, 1989).

35   *The Voice of the Mother*, as above, p. 37.

36   Sidonie Smith and Julia Watson, *Reading Autobiography: A Guide for Interpreting Life Narratives* (Minneapolis: University of Minnesota Press, 2001), p. 20.

37   Ibid., p. 37.

38   Ibid., pp. 41–42.

39   Ibid., pp. 22–23. Scriptotherapy is defined here as a phenomenon in which 'speaking or writing about trauma becomes a process through which the narrator finds words to give voice to what was previously unspeakable. And that process can be, though it is not necessarily, cathartic. Thus narrators of trauma often testify to the therapeutic effects of telling or writing a story.'

40 Tess Cosslett, *Women Writing Childbirth: Modern Discourses of Motherhood* (Manchester: Manchester University Press, 1994), p. 1.

41 Ibid., p. 4.

42 Ibid.

43 Ibid.

44 Paul Skenazy, 'Coming Home' (1989), in *Conversations with Maxine Hong Kingston*, as above, pp. 104–117; p. 123.

45 My emphasis in this section upon the no name woman's story should not distract from other manifestations of the body as a site of resistance in the text. The Fa Mu Lan parable can also be read as furthering the theme of woman-body in the text. For instance, this tale promotes the theme of women's bodies as a further site of resistance – both as a woman fighter and via the tattoos she bears upon her back.

46 Lauren Rusk, *The Life Writing of Otherness: Woolf, Baldwin, Kingston, and Winterson* (New York: Routledge, 2002), p. 84.

47 *Reading Autobiography*, as above, p. 198.

48 *The Life Writing of Otherness*, as above, p. 79.

49 Wendy Ho, *In Her Mother's House: The Politics of Asian American Mother–Daughter Writing* (Walnut Creek: Alta Mira, 1999), p. 117.

50 Ibid., p. 19.

51 King-kok Cheung, *Articulate Silences: Hisaye Yamamoto, Maxine Hong Kingston, Jooy Kogawa* (Ithaca: Cornel University Press), p. 121. Cheung also reminds us that talk-story is *both* a structure and a tradition.

52 Kingston, 'Statement of Plans', 'Maxine Hong Kingston Papers', Bancroft Library, University of California, Berkeley, p. 1.

53 'An Interview with Maxine Hong Kingston', as above, p. 11.

54 'Coming Home', as above, p. 149.

Chapter 3

1 Maxine Hong Kingston, 'The Gold Mountain Man', 'Maxine Hong Kingston Papers', Bancroft Library, University of California, Berkeley, p. 1.

2 'Maxine Hong Kingston', in Marilyn Yalom (ed.), *Women Writers*

of the West Coast: Speaking of their Lives and Careers (Santa Barbara: Capra Press, 1983), pp. 11–19; p. 14.

3 Maxine Hong Kingston, 'Statement of Plans', 'Maxine Hong Kingston Papers', Bancroft Library, University of California, Berkeley, p. 1.

4 Ibid.

5 Paula Rabinowitz (1986), 'Eccentric Memories: A Conversation with Maxine Hong Kingston', in Paul Skenazy and Tera Martin (eds), *Conversations with Maxine Hong Kingston* (Jackson: University Press of Mississippi, 1998), pp. 67–76; p. 72.

6 Kay Bonetti (1986), 'An Interview with Maxine Hong Kingston', in *Conversations with Maxine Hong Kingston*, as above, pp. 33–46; p. 39.

7 Maureen Sabine, *Maxine Hong Kingston's Broken Book of Life: An Intertextual Study of 'The Woman Warrior' and 'China Men'* (Honolulu: University of Hawai'i Press, 2004), p. 168.

8 'Statement of Plans', as above, p. 1.

9 Timothy Pfaff, (1980), 'Talk with Mrs. Kingston', in *Conversations with Maxine Hong Kingston*, as above, pp. 14–20; p. 17.

10 'Statement of Plans', as above, p. 1.

11 Maxine Hong Kingston, *China Men* (London: Picador, 1981), p. 99. All references are to this edition and hereafter are cited parenthetically in the text.

12 'Statement of Plans', as above, p. 2.

13 Ibid., p. 3.

14 Ibid.

15 I first discussed my ideas on Kingston's manipulation of the discourses of nationality and citizenship in my book *Negotiating Identities* (Manchester: Manchester University Press, 2002), pp. 180–194.

16 See Jeff Spinner, *The Boundaries of Citizenship: Race, Ethnicity, and Nationality in the Liberal State* (Baltimore: Johns Hopkins University Press, 1995), p. 168, for a discussion of the 'battle-grounds' of identity.

17 Benedict Anderson, *Imagined Communities: Reflections on the Origin and Spread of Nationalism* (London: Verso, 1991).

18 See Homi K. Bhabha, *Nation and Narration* (London: Routledge, 1990), pp. 1–6.

19 Ibid., p. 300.

20 Linda Hutcheon, *A Poetics of Postmodernism: History, Theory, Fiction* (London: Routledge, 1988), p. 56.

21 For discussions of the generic confusion surrounding Kingston's work, see LeiLani Nishime, 'Engendering Genre: Gender and Nationalism in *China Men* and *The Woman Warrior*' MELUS, 20: 1 (1995), 67–82; also Sau-ling Cynthia Wong, 'Autobiography as Guided Chinatown Tour? Maxine Hong Kingston's *The Woman Warrior* and the Chinese-American Autobiographical Controversy' in James Robert Payne (ed.), *Multicultural Autobiography: American Lives* (Knoxville: University of Tennessee Press, 1992), pp. 248–279. For perhaps the most vitriolic discussion of Kingston's use of genre, see Frank Chin, 'This Is Not an Autobiography', *Genre*, 18:2 (1985), pp. 109–130.

22 Kingston quoted in 'Talk with Mrs. Kingston', as above, p. 20.

23 This is Homi Bhabha's term; *Nation and Narration*, as above, p. 315.

24 See Sau-ling Wong's article, quoted above, for a discussion of the demand for ethnic autobiography to be representative, especially pp. 258–259.

25 This is LeiLani Nishime's phrase. The same can be seen in the 'On Fathers' section of 'Engendering Genre', an introductory piece discussing the way that 'fathers' look and behave in the same way. In 'Alaska China Men', Kingston writes that 'perhaps any China Man was China Joe' (p. 160).

26 See Donald C. Goellnicht, 'Tang Ao in America: Male Subject Positions in *China Men*', in Shirley Goek-lin Lim and Amy Ling (eds), *Reading the Literatures of Asian America* (Philadelphia: Temple University Press, 1992), pp. 191–214. Goellnicht is citing Amy Ling here, see p. 207.

27 Again, Nishime's term. See p. 74 of her article, cited above.

28 I have taken this phrase from Alfred S. Wang's article, 'Maxine Hong Kingston's Reclaiming of America: The Birthright of the Chinese-American Male', *South Dakota Review*, 26:1 (1988), 18–29.

29 Annette Kolodny, 'Letting Go Our Grand Obsessions: Notes Toward a New Literary History of the American Frontiers', in Michael Moon and Cathy Davidson (eds), *Subjects and Citizens: Nation, Race And Gender From Oroonoko To Anita Hill* (Durham: Duke University Press, 1995), pp. 9–26.

30 Ibid., p. 24.

31 Ibid., p. 13.

32 Ibid.

33 Ibid., p. 11.

34 Ibid.

35 Annette Kolodny, *The Land Before Her: Fantasy and Experience of the American Frontiers, 1630–1860* (Chapel Hill: University of North Carolina Press, 1984).

36 Ibid, p. 5.

37 'Letting Go Our Grand Obsessions', as above, p. 11.

38 *The Boundaries of Citizenship*, as above, p. 10.

39 Annette Kolodny, *The Lay of the Land: Metaphor as Experience and History in American Life and Letters* (Chapel Hill: University of North Carolina Press, 1975), p. xiii.

40 Ibid., p. ix.

41 *The Land Before Her*, as above, p. 5.

42 Ibid., p. 37; p. 237.

43 This is the story of enforced feminisation in the Land of Women; see *China Men*, pp. 9–10.

44 'Letting Go Our Grand Obsessions', as above, p. 17.

45 *The Boundaries of Citizenship*, as above, p. 10.

46 It is also significant that here the Chinese immigrant men choose the names of prominent nation-building politicians: Roosevelt and Woodrow.

47 Another example of the way that the Second World War forced Asian Americans to choose between conflicting national allegiances in this manner can be found in John Okada's novel *No-No Boy* (Seattle: University of Washington Press, 1976).

48 Once again, the name of the hall, 'Confucius Hall', is not insignificant.

49 *Imagined Communities*, as above, p. 164.

50 Ibid., p. 173.

51 *A Poetics of Postmodernism*, as above, p. 73.

52 Ibid., p. 60.

53 Kingston indicates the official status of 'The Laws' section structurally too: the 'chronology' format she adopts signals a departure from her fictional text.

54 *A Poetics of Postmodernism*, as above, p. 69.

Chapter 4

1   Anne Tyler, 'Manic Monologue', *The New Republic* 200 (17th April, 1989), pp. 44–46; p. 46.

2   Caroline Ong, 'Demons and Warriors', *Times Literary Supplement* (15th September, 1989), p. 998.

3   Pamela Longfellow, 'Monkey Wrenched', *Ms.* Magazine (17th June, 1989), p. 66.

4   Gerald Vizenor, 'Postmodern Monkey', *American Book Review* 11 (January, 1990), p. 17; p. 22.

5   Nicci Gerrard, 'Wittman Ah Sing', *The New Statesman and Society*, 2:64 (25th August, 1989), p. 28. In her essay, 'Bee-e-een! Nation, Transformation, and the Hyphen of Ethnicity in Kingston's *Tripmaster Monkey*', Isabella Furth describes the critical reaction to this book as 'almost schizophrenic' (p. 36).

6   John Leonard, 'Of Thee Ah Sing', *The Nation* (5th June, 1989), pp. 768–772; p. 768.

7   Bharati Mukherjee, 'Wittman at the Golden Gate', *The Washington Post* (16th April, 1989), p. xi.

8   E.D. Huntley, *Maxine Hong Kingston: A Critical Companion* (Westport: Greenwood Press, 2001), pp. 158–159.

9   Robert Siegle, *Suburban Ambush: Downtown Writing and the Fiction of Insurgency* (Baltimore: Johns Hopkins University Press, 1989).

10 Paul Skenazy, 'Kingston at the University', in Paul Skenazy and Tera Martin (eds), *Conversations with Maxine Hong Kingston* (Jackson: University Press of Mississippi, 1998), pp. 118–158; p. 149.

11 William Satake Blauvelt, 'Talking with the Woman Warrior', in *Conversations with Maxine Hong Kingston*, as above, pp. 77–85; p. 77.

12 In many ways, Berkeley (and San Francisco) was the epicentre of the sixties' counterculture – it was the location of the student protests and the 'Free Speech Movement', the 1967 San Francisco 'Be-In' and the hippie world of Haight-Ashbury, and spawned its own unique music, literature and festival culture.

13 Maxine Hong Kingston, *Tripmaster Monkey: His Fake Book* (London: Picador, 1989), p. 1. All references are to this edition and hereafter are cited parenthetically in the text.

14 Wittman's incessant talk has been perceived as a problem by Kingston's critics. Kingston was not unaware of this potential problem. In a letter written during the re-drafting of *Tripmaster*,

Kingston's editor at Alfred A. Knopf warned her that 'Wittman, to put it bluntly, is in danger of wearing out his welcome from time to time – long before the end' (Letter to Kingston, 13th April, 1987; Maxine Hong Kingston Papers, Bancroft Library, University of California, Berkeley).

15 Shelley Fisher Fishkin, 'Interview with Maxine Hong Kingston', in *Conversations with Maxine Hong Kingston*, as above, pp. 159–167; p. 160.

16 Kingston has reminisced that it was often *her* role to be the trippers' guide.

17 Yan Gao, *The Art of Parody: Maxine Hong Kingston's Use of Chinese Sources* (New York: Peter Lang, 1996), p. 99.

18 C.T. Hsia, *The Classic Chinese Novel* (New York: Columbia University Press, 1968), p. 2; p. 133.

19 *The Art of Parody*, p. 100.

20 The title page of the first American edition of *Tripmaster Monkey* included a Chinese cartoon illustration of Monkey King, which emphasised Monkey's agility and playfulness.

21 Diane Simmons, *Maxine Hong Kingston* (New York: Twayne, 1998), p. 98.

22 Amy Ling, *Between Worlds: Women Writers of Chinese Ancestry* (New York: Pergamon, 1990).

23 'Talking with the Woman Warrior', as above, p. 78.

24 Quoted in *The Art of Parody*, as above, p. 144.

25 *The Classic Chinese Novel*, as above, p. 135.

26 'Talking with the Woman Warrior', as above, p. 82.

27 See *The Classic Chinese Novel*, p. 9 for a discussion of this.

28 John Fowles, *The French Lieutenant's Woman* (New York: Little Brown, 1969), p. 292.

29 Linda Hutcheon, *The Politics of Postmodernism* (New York: Routledge, 1989), p. 51.

30 Jody Hoy, 'To Be Able to See the Tao', in *Conversations with Maxine Hong Kingston*, as above, pp. 47–66; p. 51.

31 Tricksters are shape-shifting, cunning characters who exist on the borders of society.

32 Jeanne Rosier Smith, *Writing Tricksters: Mythic Gambols in American Ethnic Literature* (Berkeley: University of California Press, 1997), p. 49.

33 Ibid., pp. 48–49.

34 William Hynes, 'Inconclusive Conclusions: Tricksters – Meta-players and Revealers', in William Doty and William Hynes (eds), *Mythical Trickster Figures* (Tuscaloosa: University of Alabama Press, 1993), pp. 202–217; p. 216.

35 *The Classic Chinese Novel*, as above, p. 35.

36 Ibid., p. 75.

37 Ibid., pp. 75–76.

38 Ibid., p. 76; p. 71.

39 Diane Simmons, *Maxine Hong Kingston*, as above, p. 160.

40 'Trip' can be a journey, experience, hallucinogenic episode, mistake and game. See also *The Art of Parody*, pp. 140–141.

41 Marilyn Chin, 'Writing the Other: A Conversation with Maxine Hong Kingston', in *Conversations with Maxine Hong Kingston*, as above, pp. 86–103; p. 140.

42 See 'Bee-e-een!', cited above.

43 In her proposed plans for the book, Kingston noted that Wittman would 'further the theme of the alienated comic hero. Witman [sic] Ah Sing constantly tries to disrupt human society'. 'Plans' (1981), 'Maxine Hong Kingston Papers', Bancroft Library, University of California, Berkeley, p. 1.

44 Maxine Hong Kingston, 'An Icicle in the Desert', *Through the Black Curtain* (Berkeley: Bancroft Library, 1987), p. 11.

45 'Talking with the Woman Warrior', as above, p. 78.

46 Ibid., p. 142.

47 'Writing the Other', as above, p. 61.

48 *Tripmaster Monkey* was originally entitled 'MONKEY'S PATTER SONG AND FAKE BOOK'. Kingston wrote that the 'patter song' refers to Wittman's heritage and vocation, as he came 'from a long line of theater people'. In the same piece, she also noted: 'another way I have garnered information on the theater is that my husband, Earll, and my son, Joseph, are both actors; my brother and sister-in-law and their three children work behind the scenes. Thus, like my hero, I come from a theater family'. 'Plans', 1981, as above, p. 1.

49 Diane Simmons, *Maxine Hong Kingston*, as above, p. 152.

50 Theodore Roszak, *The Making of a Counterculture* (Berkeley: University of California Press, 1968), p. xxxiii.

51 Ibid., p. 143.

52 A. Noelle Williams, 'Parody and Pacifist Transformations in Maxine Hong Kingston's *Tripmaster Monkey: His Fake Book*', *MELUS*, 20:1 (Spring, 1995), 83–100; p. 88. In their readings of *Tripmaster Monkey* both Jeanne Rosier Smith and A. Noelle Williams draw heavily upon Henry Louis Gates' notion of 'signifying' as a parodic technique (in the sense of 'motivated repetition and revision'), as a common feature of trickster texts. See *Writing Tricksters*, as above, pp. 14–16; 'Parody and Pacifist Transformations', as above, p. 88.

53 Ibid., p. 88.

54 There are other hints that Kingston modelled Wittman on Chin. In notes written while she was writing *Tripmaster*, Kingston says 'And Frank Chin is the box, the claustrophobia, the twisty face, the fear, the stunted male. Will it be possible to begin with him and yet fly?' ('Maxine Hong Kingston Papers', as above, 10th July, 1980, p. 2).

55 Frank Chin, Letter to Kingston, *ibid.*, 22nd October, 1976, p. 5.

56 Frank Chin, Letter to Kingston, *ibid.*, 2nd September, 1976, p. 2.

57 Frank Chin, Letter to Kingston, *ibid.*, 27th October, 1976, p. 18; p. 23.

58 'Talking with the Woman Warrior', as above, p. 77.

59 'Plans', as above, p. 1.

60 Debra Shostak, 'Maxine Hong Kingston's Fake Books', in Amritjit Singh, Joseph T. Skerrett and Robert E. Hogan (eds), *Memory, Narrative, and Identity: New Essays in Ethnic American Literatures* (Boston: Northeastern University Press, 1994), pp. 233–260; pp. 239–240.

61 Shelley Fisher Fishkin, 'Interview with Maxine Hong Kingston', in *Conversations with Maxine Hong Kingston*, as above, pp. 159–167; p. 164.

62 'Plans', as above, pp. 2–3.

63 Sau-ling Cynthia Wong, 'Ethnic Subject, Ethnic Sign, and the Difficulty of Rehabilitative Representation: Chinatown in Some Works of Chinese American Fiction', in *The Yearbook of English Studies*, 24 (1994), pp. 251–262; p. 251.

64 William Boelhower, *Through a Glass Darkly: Ethnic Semiosis in American Literature* (Oxford: Oxford University Press, 1987).

65 'Ethnic Subject, Ethnic Sign', as above, p. 251.

66 Ibid., p. 252.

67   Ibid.

68   Ibid.

69   Ibid.

70   Ibid., p. 253.

71   Elaine Kim, *Asian American Literature: An Introduction to the Writings and their Social Context* (Philadelphia: Temple University Press, 1982), p. 21.

72   Joseph Rothschild, *Ethnopolitics: A Conceptual Framework* (New York: Columbia University Press, 1981), p. 63.

73   *Between Worlds: Women Writers of Chinese Ancestry*, as above, p. 10.

74   I have previously discussed Wittman's treatise on racism and stereotyping in my book *Negotiating Identities* (Manchester: Manchester University Press, 2002). See chapter four, 'Writing Biraciality'.

Chapter 5

1   Maxine Hong Kingston, *Hawai'i One Summer* (1987; Honolulu: University of Hawai'i Press, 1998). All references are to this edition and hereafter are cited parenthetically in the text.

2   Gary Kubota, 'Interview with Maxine Hong Kingston', 1977, in Paul Skenazy and Tera Martin (eds), *Conversations with Maxine Hong Kingston* (Jackson: University Press of Mississippi, 1998), pp. 1–4; p. 4.

3   Diane Simmons, *Maxine Hong Kingston* (New York: Twayne, 1999), p. 22.

4   Another important factor which informs and influences the text is that while resident on the islands, Kingston wrote *China Men*, so this is actually an important co-text to *Hawai'i One Summer*.

5   Jody Hoy, 'To Be Able to See the Tao', in *Conversations with Maxine Hong Kingston*, as above, pp. 47–66; p. 53.

6   Paul Skenazy, 'Coming Home', in *Conversations with Maxine Hong Kingston*, as above, pp. 104–117; p. 113.

7   For a cogent summary of the critical debates which circulate around the dichotomy of local/global, see Miranda Joseph, 'The Discourse of Global/Localization', in Arnaldo Cruz-Malavé and Martin F. Manalansan (eds), *Queer Globalizations: Citizenship and the*

Afterlife of Colonialism (New York: New York University Press, 2002), pp. 71–99. See also, Lisa Lowe, *Immigrant Acts: On Asian American Cultural Politics* (Durham and London: Duke University Press, 1996).

8   'The Discourse of Global/Localization', as above, p. 72.

9   Stephen Sumida, *And the View From the Shore: Literary Traditions of Hawai'i* (Seattle: University of Washington Press, 1991), p. xvi.

10   'Coming Home', as above, p. 113.

11   Ibid., p. 116.

12   Ibid., p. 112.

13   Timothy Pfaff, 'Talk with Mrs Kingston' (1980), in *Conversations with Maxine Hong Kingston*, pp. 14–20; p. 15.

14   Karen Horton, 'Honolulu Interview' (1979), in ibid., pp. 513; p. 10.

15   'To Be Able to See the Tao', in ibid., p. 53.

16   *And the View From the Shore*, as above, p. xi.

17   Ibid., pp. xiv; xvi; vviii.

18   Ibid., p. xvi.

19   Stephen Sumida, 'Postcolonialism, Nationalism, and the Emergence of Asian/Pacific American Literatures', in King-kok Cheung (ed.), *An Interethnic Companion to Asian American Literature* (Cambridge: Cambridge University Press, 1997), pp. 274–288; p. 277.

20   Rachel C. Lee, 'Asian American Short Fiction', in Sau-ling Cynthia Wong and Stephen H. Sumida (eds), *A Resource Guide to Asian American Literature* (New York: MLA, 2001), pp. 252–284; p. 262. Of course, these categories are not fixed, as I detail below with reference to alternative categories of 'tourist' versus 'local'.

21   Eric Chock and Darrell H.Y. Lum (eds), *The Best of Bamboo Ridge: The Hawai'i Writers' Quarterly* (Honolulu: Bamboo Ridge, 1986), p. 4.

22   Deborah L. Madsen, *Maxine Hong Kingston* (New York: Gale, 2000), p. 80.

23   A 'tourist' perspective is the opposite of 'local' in the Hawai'ian lexicon, as Sumida notes; see *And the View From the Shore*, as above, p. 225. There is a third tradition, too, which Sumida characterises as a 'colonial' perspective, see p. 238.

24   Noël Sturgeon, 'The Nature of Race', in Karen J. Warren (ed.), *Ecofeminism: Women, Culture, Nature* (Bloomington: Indiana University Press, 1997), pp. 260–278; p. 263.

25   Ibid.

26   Maria Mies and Vandana Shiva, *Ecofeminism* (London: Zed Books, 1993), p. 13.

27   Gretchen T. Legler, 'Ecofeminist Literary Criticism', in *Ecofeminism*, as above, pp. 227–238; p. 229; p. 233.

28   Kingston describes a similar incident in *China Men*, where the great-grandfather sees the dead warriors too.

29   Diane Simmons, *Maxine Hong Kingston*, p. 21.

30   *And the View from the Shore*, as above, p. 239; p. 244.

31   Frank Chin, 'The Most Popular Book in China', *Quilt* 4, edited by Ishmael Reed and Al Young (Berkeley: Quilt, 1984), p. 10.

32   Maxine Hong Kingston, *China Men*, pp. 89–90.

33   Ibid., pp. 90–92.

Chapter 6

1   Maxine Hong Kingston, *To Be the Poet* (Cambridge, Mass.: Harvard University Press, 2002), p. 1. Hereafter references to this are cited in parentheses in the text.

2   Maxine Hong Kingston, *The Fifth Book of Peace* (New York: Knopf, 2003), p. 241. Hereafter references to this are cited in parentheses in the text.

3   The ways Kingston's book intersects with US Vietnam literature are complex. Fictional and autobiographical output on the subject of Vietnam is vast, but other 'auto/fictional' writings for peace notably include: *Kontum Diary: Captured Writings Bring Peace to a Vietnam Veteran* by Paul Reed (Chicago: Summit Publishing Group, 1996); *Patriotism, Peace, and Vietnam: A Memoir* by Peggy Hanna (Springfield, Ohio: Left to Write, 2003); *Harmless as Doves: Witnessing for Peace in Vietnam* by Mary Sue Rosenberger (Elgin, Illinois: Brethren Press, 1988); and other notable fictional texts include *In the Lake of the Woods* by Tim O'Brien (New York: Penguin, 1995; O'Brien has been acknowledged by Kingston to be a role model); Michael Herr's *Dispatches* (New York: Vintage, 1968), and Philip Caputo's *A Rumor of War* (New York: Holt, 1977). As I later discuss, two works perhaps closest to Kingston's own are Le Ly Hayslip's *When Heaven and Earth Changed Places* (New York: Doubleday, 1989) and *Child of*

War, Woman of Peace (New York: Doubleday, 1993), since Hayslip is also Asian American (Vietnamese American), and both writers seek to counter the US-centric conceptualisation of Vietnam as two countries. Several of Kingston's own veteran students have written and published memoirs as a result of their work with her too. See for example John Mulligan, *Shopping Cart Soldiers* (St. Paul, Minneapolis: Curbstone Press, 1997).

4 Gabriel Kolko, *Vietnam: Anatomy of a Peace* (New York: Routledge, 1997), p. 1.

5 Kingston, 'Interview with Neila C. Seshachari' (1993), in Paul Skenazy and Tera Martin (eds), *Conversations with Maxine Hong Kingston* (Jackson: University Press of Mississippi, 1998), pp. 192–214; p. 196.

6 Mark Baker (ed.), *Nam: The Vietnam War in the Words of the Men and Women Who Fought There* (New York: Rowman and Littlefield, 1981), p. 17.

7 The 'teach-ins' involved all-night teaching sessions on Vietnam held by war critics. In effect they became anti-war rallies.

8 Diane Simmons, *Maxine Hong Kingston* (New York: Twayne, 1999), p. 3.

9 'Interview with Neila Seshachari', as above, p. 223.

10 Virginia Woolf, *Three Guineas* (1938; London: Penguin, 1977), p. 143.

11 Peggy Kamuf, quoted in Marie-Luise Gättens, *Women Writers and Facism: Reconstructing History* (Gainsville: University Press of Florida, 1995), p. 35. Kamuf goes on to assert that women writers' response to war is often to produce memoirs as this form insists upon historical presence and bears witness in some way, thus eschewing the whimsicality of imaginative fiction. Thus memoir becomes a means of challenging the present rather than simply recounting the past by 'the remembered ... with the imagined' as Kingston does in *The Fifth Book of Peace* (p. 78; p. 170). For an alternative discussion of this subject, see Miriam Cooke and Angela Woollacott (eds), *Gendering War Talk* (Princeton: Princeton University Press, 1993) and Catherine Marshall, *Militarism versus Feminism: Writings on Women and War* (London: Virago, 1987).

12 In fact, Kingston also lost the ability to read as well. In a 1996 interview, she said: 'I lost my ability to read. The same thing happened to my husband Earll – we just couldn't read. It was one of my symptoms of post-traumatic stress disorder. I wasn't able to concentrate. Even the newspaper – I couldn't get past the first

paragraph' ('As Truthful as Possible: An Interview with Maxine Hong Kingston', Eric J. Schroeder, 1996, *Conversations with Maxine Hong Kingston*, as above, pp. 215–228; p. 222).

13 Kingston, 'Interview with Donna Perry', in ibid., pp. 168–188; p. 169.

14 Kingston, 'Interview with Gary Kubota', in ibid., pp. 1–4; p. 3.

15 'Interview with Neila Seshachari', as above, p. 194.

16 Robert J. Topmiller, *The Lotus Unleashed: The Buddhist Peace Movement in South Vietnam, 1964–1966* (Knoxville: University Press of Kentucky, 2002), pp. 8–9. Thich Nhat Hanh fled South Vietnam in 1966 after a failed attempt on his life. He then travelled through nineteen countries promoting peace, and spoke with Robert McNamara, Pope Paul VI and Martin Luther King, Jr, amongst others. Martin Luther King actually nominated him for the Nobel Peace Prize (*The Lotus Unleashed*, as above, p. 138). Topmiller describes his legacy: 'The monk's courageous stand meant that he could not return to South Vietnam; his life would be in constant danger for calling for reconciliation in a country exhausted and sickened by decades of conflict' (ibid., p. 123). For more on Thich Nhat Hanh's teachings, see his *Peace is Every Step: The Path of Mindfulness in Everyday Life* (New York: Bantam, 1992), and *Vietnam: Lotus in a Sea of Fire* (New York: Hill and Wang, 1967). Among the best histories of Vietnam and the antiwar movement are: George Herring, *America's Longest War: America and Vietnam* (New York: Mcgraw-Hill, 1985) and for the alternative perspective, *A Vietcong Memoir: An Inside Account of the Vietnam War and Its Aftermath* by Troung Nhu Tang (New York: Vintage, 1986). On the Buddhist peace movement, see *The Lotus Unleashed*, as above.

17 'Interview with Neila Seshachari', as above, p. 196.

18 Leslie Bow, 'Third World Testimony in the Era of Globalization: Vietnam, Sexual Trauma and Le Ly Hayslip's Art of Neutrality', in W.S. Hesford and W. Kozol (eds), *Haunting Violations: Feminist Criticism and the Crisis of the Real* (Urbana: University of Illinois Press, 2001), pp. 178–179.

19 Angela K. Smith (ed.), *Gender and Warfare in the Twentieth Century* (Manchester: Manchester University Press, 2004), p. 4.

20 Ibid., p. 176.

21 William Cloonan, *The Writing of War: French and German Fiction and World War II* (Jacksonville: University Press of Florida, 1999), pp. 71–72.

Chapter 7

1 For details of these, and the other, books mentioned here, please see the Select Bibliography.

2 See Sau-ling C. Wong, 'Denationalization Reconsidered: Asian American Cultural Criticism at a Theoretical Crossroads', *Amerasia*, 21:1 and 2 (1995), 1–27.

3 For concise discussions of Asian American feminist critiques of Asian American nationalism, see Jinqi Ling, *Narrating National-isms: Ideology and Form in Asian American Literature* (New York: Oxford University Press, 1998), chapter five; David Leiwei Li, *Imagining the Nation: Asian American Literature and Cultural Consent* (Stanford: Stanford University Press, 1998), part one.

Select bibliography

Works by Maxine Hong Kingston

FICTION AND LIFE-WRITING

The Woman Warrior: Memoirs of a Girlhood among Ghosts, New York, Knopf, 1976. (London, Allen Lane, 1977)
China Men, New York, Knopf, 1980. (London, Pan, 1981)
Tripmaster Monkey: His Fake Book, New York, Knopf, 1989. (London: Pan, 1989)
The Fifth Book of Peace, New York, Knopf, 2003.

NON-FICTION

Hicks, Jack, James D. Houston, Maxine Hong Kingston and Al Young (eds), *Literature of California, I: Native American Beginnings to 1945*, Berkeley, University of California Press, 2000.
Kingston, Maxine Hong, *Hawai'i One Summer, 1978*, San Francisco, Meadow Press, 1987. (Honolulu, University of Hawai'i Press, 1987 (1998))
——, *Through the Black Curtain*, Berkeley, The Friends of the Bancroft Library, University of California, 1987.
——, *To be the Poet*, Cambridge, Harvard University Press, 2002.

ARTICLES, INTRODUCTIONS, PUBLISHED SPEECHES

Allende, Isabel, Barry Gifford and Maxine Hong Kingston, 'The Holly-wood Shuffle', *San Francisco Review of Books*, 20:1 (1995), 30.
Bonetti, Kay, 'Maxine Hong Kingston Interview with Kay Bonetti', Columbia, American Audio Prose Library, 1986. Cassette 53 mins.
Kingston, Maxine Hong, 'Cultural Mis-Reading by American Reviewers', in Guy Amirthanayagam (ed.), *Asian and Western*

Writers in Dialogue: New Cultural Identities, London, Macmillan, 1982, pp. 55–65.

——, 'Personal Statement', in Shirley Geok-lin Lim (ed.), *Approaches to Teaching Kingston's* The Woman Warrior, New York, Modern Language Association of America, 1991, pp. 23–25.

——, 'The Novel's Next Step: From the Novel of the Americas to the Global Novel', in Raymond Leslie Williams, *The Novel in the Americas*, Niwot, University Press of Colorado, 1992, pp. 13–18.

——, 'A Letter to Garrett Hongo upon the Publication of *The Open Boat*', *Amerasia Journal*, 20:3 (1994), 25.

——, 'Finding a Voice', in Virginia P. Clark, Paul A. Eschholz and Alfred F. Rosa, *Language: Readings in Language and Culture*, New York, St. Martin's, 1998, pp. 13–18.

——, 'Stories My Country Told Me', Princeton, Films for the Humanities, 1966 (2000). VHS 53 mins.

Moyers, Bill D., *A World of Ideas*, Alexandria, PBS Video, 1990. VHS 56 mins.

—— and Leslie Clark (prod.), *The Stories of Maxine Hong Kingston*, Princeton, Films for the Humanities, 1994. VHS 60 mins.

Walkinshaw, Jean and Gary Gibson, *Westwords: Six Western Writers*, Alexandria, PBS Video, 1996. VHS 57 mins.

Wright, Charles, Barry Lopez and Maxine Kingston, 'A Chinese Garland', *North American Review*, 273:3 (1988), 38–42.

Criticism

BOOKS

Cheung, King-kok, *Articulate Silences: Hisaye Yamamoto, Maxine Hong Kingston, Joy Kogawa*, Ithaca, Cornell University Press, 1993.

Crow, Charles L., *Maxine Hong Kingston*. Boise, Boise State University Press, 2004.

Eakin, Paul John, *Fictions in Autobiography: Studies in the Art of Self-Invention*, Princeton, Princeton University Press, 1985.

Feng, Pin-chia, *The Female* Bildungsroman *by Toni Morrison and Maxine Hong Kingston: A Postmodern Reading*, New York, Peter Lang, 1997.

Gao, Yan, *The Art of Parody: Maxine Hong Kingston's Use of Chinese Sources*, New York, Peter Lang, 1996.

Ho, Wendy, *In Her Mother's House: The Politics of Asian American Mother–Daughter Writing*, Walnut Creek, AltaMira, 1999.

Hoeveler, Diane Long, and Janet K. Boles (eds), *Women of Color: Defining the Issues, Hearing the Voices*, Westport, Greenwood, 2001.

Huntley, E. D., *Maxine Hong Kingston: A Critical Companion*, Westport, Greenwood, 2001.

Lim, Shirley Geok-lin (ed.), *Approaches to Teaching Kingston's* The Woman Warrior, New York, Modern Language Association of America, 1991.

Ludwig, Sami, *Concrete Language: Intercultural Communication in Maxine Hong Kingston's* The Woman Warrior *and Ishmael Reed's* Mumbo Jumbo, Frankfurt, Peter Lang, 1996.

Ma, Sheng Mei, *The Deathly Embrace: Orientalism and Asian American Identity*, Minneapolis, University of Minnesota Press, 2000.

Simmons, Diane, *Maxine Hong Kingston*, New York, Twayne, 1999.

Sitesh, Aruna, *Her Testimony: American Women Writers of the 90s in Conversation with Aruna Sitesh*, New Delhi, Affiliated East-West, 1994.

Skenazy, Paul, and Tera Martin (eds), *Conversations with Maxine Hong Kingston*, Jackson, University Press of Mississippi, 1998.

Smith, Jeanne Rosier, *Writing Tricksters: Mythic Gambols in American Ethnic Literature*, Berkeley, University of California Press, 1997.

Wogowitsch, Margit, *Narrative Strategies and Multicultural Identity: Maxine Hong Kingston in Context*, Vienna, Braumuller, 1995.

Wong, Sau-ling Cynthia, *Reading Asian American Literature: From Necessity to Extravagance*, Princeton, Princeton University Press, 1993.

——, *Maxine Hong Kingston's* The Woman Warrior: *A Casebook*, New York, Oxford University Press, 1999.

ARTICLES AND ESSAYS

Adams, Timothy Dow, 'Talking Stories/Telling Lies in *The Woman Warrior*', in Shirley Geok-lin Lim (ed.), *Approaches to Teaching Kingston's* The Woman Warrior, New York, Modern Language Association of America, 1991, pp. 151–157.

Allen, Joseph R., 'Dressing and Undressing the Chinese Woman Warrior', *Positions: East Asia Cultures Critique*, 4:2 (1996), 343–379.

Aubrey, James R., 'Woman Warriors and Military Students', in Shirley Geok-lin Lim (ed.), *Approaches to Teaching Kingston's* The Woman Warrior, New York, Modern Language Association of America, 1991, pp. 80–86.

Bacchilega, Cristina, 'Feminine Voices Inscribing Sarraute's *Childhood* and Kingston's *Woman Warrior*', *Textual Practice*, 6:1 (1992), 101–118.

Baer, Elizabeth, 'The Confrontation of East and West: *The Woman Warrior* as Postmodern Autobiography', *Redneck Review of Literature*, 21 (1991), 26–29.

Barker-Nunn, Jeanne, 'Telling the Mother's Story: History and Connection in the Autobiographies of Maxine Hong Kingston and Kim Chernin', *Women's Studies: An Interdisciplinary Journal*, 14:1 (1987), 55–63.

Begum, Khani, 'Confirming the Place of "The Other": Gender and Ethnic Identity in Maxine Hong Kingston's *The Woman Warrior*', in Regina Barreca (ed.), *New Perspectives on Women and Comedy*, Philadelphia, Gordon and Breach, 1992, pp. 143–156.

Bischoff, Joan, 'Fellow Rebels: Annie Dillard and Maxine Hong Kingston', *English Journal*, 78:8 (1989), 62–67.

Bizzini, Silvia Caporale, 'Sara Suleri's *Meatless Days* and Maxine Hong Kingston's *The Woman Warrior*: Writing, History and the Self after Foucault', *Women: A Cultural Review*, 7:1 (1996), 55–65.

Blauvelt, William Satake, 'Talking with the Woman Warrior', in Paul Skenazy and Tera Martin (eds), *Conversations with Maxine Hong Kingston*, Jackson, University Press of Mississippi, 1998, pp. 77–85.

Blinde, Patricia Lin, 'The Icicle in the Desert: Perspective and Form in the Works of Two Chinese-American Women Writers', *MELUS*, 6:3 (1979), 51–71.

Bloom, Lynn Z., 'Heritages: Dimensions of Mother–Daughter Relationships in Women's Autobiographies', in Cathy N. Davidson and E. M. Broner (eds), *The Lost Tradition: Mothers and Daughters in Literature*, New York, Ungar, 1980, pp. 291–303.

Boardman, Kathleen A., 'Voice and Vision: *The Woman Warrior* in the Writing Class', in Shirley Geok-lin Lim (ed.), *Approaches to Teaching Kingston's* The Woman Warrior, New York, Modern Language Association of America, 1991, pp. 87–92.

Bonetti, Kay, 'An Interview with Maxine Hong Kingston', in Paul Skenazy and Tera Martin (eds), *Conversations with Maxine Hong Kingston*, Jackson, University Press of Mississippi, 1998, pp. 33–46.

Bow, Leslie, *Betrayal and Other Acts of Subversion: Feminism, Sexual Politics, Asian American Women's Literature*, Princeton: Princeton University Press, 2001.

Brownmiller, Susan, 'Susan Brownmiller Talks with Maxine Hong Kingston: Author of The Woman Warrior', in Sau-ling Cynthia Wong (ed.), *Maxine Hong Kingston's* The Woman Warrior: A Casebook, New York, Oxford University Press, 1999, pp. 173–179.

Buss, Helen M., 'Reading for the Doubled Discourse of American Women's Autobiography', *A/B: Auto/Biography Studies*, 6:1 (1991), 95–108.

——, 'Memoir with an Attitude: One Reader Reads *The Woman*

Warrior: Memoirs of a Girlhood among Ghosts', *A/B: Auto/ Biography Studies*, 12:2 (1997), 203–224.

Chang, Hsiao-hung, 'Gender Crossing in Maxine Hong Kingston's *Tripmaster'*, *MELUS*, 22:1 (1997), 15–34.

Chen, Victoria, 'Chinese American Women, Language, and Moving Subjectivity', *Women and Language*, 18:1 (1995), 3–7.

Cheung, Kai-chong, 'Maxine Hong Kingston's Non-Chinese Man', *Tamkang Review: A Quarterly of Comparative Studies between Chinese and Foreign Literatures*, 23:1–4 (1992–1993), 421–430.

Cheung, King-kok, '"Don't Tell": Imposed Silences in *The Color Purple* and *The Woman Warrior'*, *PMLA*, 103:2 (1988), 162–174. Reprinted in Janet Simpson Madden and Sara Blake (eds), *Emerging Voices*, Fort Worth, Holt, Rinehart, Winston, 1990, pp. 400–421.

——, *'The Woman Warrior* versus The Chinaman Pacific: Must a Chinese American Critic Choose between Feminism and Heroism?'*, in Marianne Hirsch and Evelyn Fox Keller (eds), *Conflicts in Feminism*, New York, Routledge, 1990, pp. 234–251. Reprinted in Sau-ling Cynthia Wong (ed.), *Maxine Hong Kingston's* The Woman Warrior: *A Casebook*, New York, Oxford University Press, 1999, pp. 113–133.

——, 'Self-Fulfilling Visions in *The Woman Warrior* and *Thousand Pieces of Gold'*, *Biography: An Interdisciplinary Quarterly*, 13:2 (1990), 143–153.

——, 'Talk Story: Counter-Memory in Maxine Hong Kingston's *China Men'*, *Tamkang Review: A Quarterly of Comparative Studies between Chinese and Foreign Literatures*, 24:1 (1993), 21–37.

—— (ed), *An Interethnic Companion to Asian American Literature*, New York, Cambridge Universit Press, 1997.

——, 'Of Men and Men: Reconstructing Chinese American Masculinity', in Sandra Kumamoto Stanley (ed.), *Other Sisterhoods: Literary Theory and U.S. Women of Color*, Urbana: University of Illinois Press, 1998, pp. 183–199.

Chin, Frank, 'The Most Popular Book in China', in Sau-ling Cynthia Wong (ed.), *Maxine Hong Kingston's* The Woman Warrior: *A Casebook*, New York, Oxford University Press, 1999, pp. 23–28.

Chin, Marilyn, 'A Melus Interview: Maxine Hong Kingston', *MELUS*, 16:4 (1989–1990), 57–74. Reprinted as 'Writing the Other: A Conversation with Maxine Hong Kingston', in Paul Skenazy and Tera Martin (eds), *Conversations with Maxine Hong Kingston*, Jackson, University Press of Mississippi, 1998, pp. 86–103.

Chin, Woon Ping, 'Children of the Chinese Diaspora: A Comparison of Lee Kok Liang's *Flowers in the Sky* and Maxine Hong Kingston's *China Men'*, in Shirley Hune, Hyung-chan Kim, Stephen S. Fugita and Amy Ling (eds), *Asian Americans: Comparative and*

Global Perspectives, Pullman, Washington State University Press, 1991, pp. 265–275.

Chiu, Jeannie, 'Fox Spirits in Hualing Nieh's *Mulberry and Peach* and Maxine Hong Kingston's *China Men*', *Notes on Contemporary Literature*, 33:1 (2003), 3–5.

Chiu, Monica, 'Being Human in the Wor(l)d: Chinese Men and Maxine Hong Kingston's Reworking of Robinson Crusoe', *Journal of American Studies*, 34:2 (2000), 187–206.

——, *Filthy Fictions: Asian American Literature by Women*, Walnut Creek, California, Alta Mira Press, 2004.

Chu, Patricia, '"The Invisible World the Emigrants Built": Cultural Self-Inscription and the Antiromantic Plots of *The Woman Warrior*', *Diaspora: A Journal of Transnational Studies*, 2:1 (1992), 95–115.

Chu, Patricia P., '*Tripmaster Monkey*, Frank Chin, and the Chinese Heroic Tradition', *Arizona Quarterly: A Journal of American Literature, Culture, and Theory*, 53:3 (1997), 117–139.

——, '*The Woman Warrior: Memoir of a Girlhood among Ghosts* by Maxine Hong Kingston', in Sau-ling Cynthia Wong and Stephen H. Sumida (eds), *A Resource Guide to Asian American Literature*, New York, Modern Language Association of America, 2001, pp. 86–96.

Chua, Cheng Lok, 'Golden Mountain: Chinese Versions of the American Dream in Lin Yutang, Louis Chu, and Maxine Hong Kingston', *Ethnic Groups*, 4:1–2 (1982), 33–59.

——, 'Mythopoesis East and West in *The Woman Warrior*', in Shirley Geok-lin Lim (ed.), *Approaches to Teaching Kingston's* The Woman Warrior, New York, Modern Language Association of America, 1991, pp. 146–150.

Chun, Gloria, 'The High Note of the Barbarian Reed Pipe: Maxine Hong Kingston', *JEthS*, 19:3 (1991), 85–94.

Cliff, Michele, 'The Making of Americans: Maxine Hong Kingston's *Crossover Dreams*', Village Voice Literary Supplement, 74 (1989), 11–13.

Cook, Rufus, 'Maintaining the Past: Cultural Continuity in Maxine Hong Kingston's Work', *Tamkang Review: A Quarterly of Comparative Studies between Chinese and Foreign Literatures*, 25:1 (1994), 35–58.

Couser, G. Thomas, 'Maxine Hong Kingston: The Auto/Biographer as Ghost-Writer', in Carol Ramelb (ed.), *Biography: East and West: Selected Conference Papers*, Honolulu, University of Hawai'i Press, 1989, pp. 231–237.

Crafton, Lisa Plummer, '"We Are Going to Carve Revenge on Your Back": Language, Culture, and the Female Body in Kingston's *The*

Woman Warrior', in Susan Shifrin (ed.), *Women as Sites of Culture: Women's Roles in Cultural Formation from the Renaissance to the Twentieth Century*, Aldershot, Ashgate, 2002, pp. 51–63.

Crow, Charles L., 'Maxine Hong Kingston', in Max Westbrook and Dan Flores (eds), *Updating the Literary West*, Fort Worth, Western Literature Association, in association with Texas Christian University Press, 1997, pp. 360–366.

Cummins, Walter, '"They Fancied Themselves Free": Exploration and Individualism', *Weber Studies: An Interdisciplinary Humanities Journal*, 11:2 (1994), 137–147.

Danahay, Martin A., 'Breaking the Silence: Symbolic Violence and the Teaching of Contemporary "Ethnic" Autobiography', *College Literature*, 18:3 (1991), 64–79.

Dasenbrock, Reed Way, 'Intelligibility and Meaningfulness in Multicultural Literature in English', *PMLA*, 102:1 (1987), 10–19. Reprinted in Sau-ling Cynthia Wong (ed.), *Maxine Hong Kingston's* The Woman Warrior: *A Casebook*, New York, Oxford University Press, 1999, pp. 159–169.

Dearborn, Mary V., *Pocahontas's Daughters: Gender and Ethnicity in American Culture*, New York, Oxford University Press, 1986.

Deeney, John J., 'Of Monkeys and Butterflies: Transformation in M. H. Kingston's *Tripmaster Monkey* and D. H. Hwang's *M. Butterfly*', *MELUS*, 18:4 (1993–1994), 21–39.

Demetrakopoulos, Stephanie A., 'The Metaphysics of Matrilinearism in Women's Autobiography: Studies of Mead's *Blackberry Winter*, Hellman's *Pentimento*, Angelou's *I Know Why the Caged Bird Sings*, and Kingston's *The Woman Warrior*', in Estelle Jelinek (ed.), *Women's Autobiography: Essays in Criticism*, Bloomington, Indiana University Press, 1980, pp. 180–205.

Donaldson, Mara E., 'Woman as Hero in Margaret Atwood's *Surfacing* and Maxine Hong Kingston's *The Woman Warrior*', in Pat Browne (ed.), *Heroines of Popular Culture*, Bowling Green, OH, Popular, 1987, pp. 101–113.

Duncan, Patti L., 'The Uses of Silence: Notes on the "Will to Unsay"', in Diane Long Hoeveler and Janet K. Boles (eds), *Women of Color: Defining the Issues, Hearing the Voices*, Westport, Greenwood, 2001, pp. 21–44.

——, *Tell this Silence: Asian American Women Writers and the Politics of Speech*, Iowa City, University of Iowa Press, 2004.

Eakin, Paul John, 'Narration and Chronology as Structures of Reference and the New Model Autobiographer', in James Olney (ed.), *Studies in Autobiography*, New York, Oxford University Press, 1988, pp. 32–41.

Fichtelberg, Joseph, 'Poet and Patriarch in Maxine Hong Kingston's

China Men', in Shirley Neuman (ed.), *Autobiography and Questions of Gender*, London, Cass, 1992, pp. 166–185.

Fishkin, Shelley Fisher, 'Interview with Maxine Hong Kingston', *American Literary History*, 3:4 (1991), 782–791. Reprinted in Paul Skenazy and Tera Martin (eds), *Conversations with Maxine Hong Kingston*, Jackson, University Press of Mississippi, 1998, pp. 159–167.

Fong, Bobby, 'Maxine Hong Kingston's Autobiographical Strategy in *The Woman Warrior*', *Biography: An Interdisciplinary Quarterly*, 12:2 (1989), 116–126.

Friedman, Susan Stanford, 'Women's Autobiographical Selves: Theory and Practice', in Shari Benstock (ed.), *The Private Self: Theory and Practice of Women's Autobiographical Writings*, Chapel Hill, University of North Carolina Press, 1988, pp. 34–62.

Frye, Joanne S., '*The Woman Warrior*: Claiming Narrative Power, Recreating Female Selfhood', in Alice Kessler-Harris and William McBrien (eds), *Faith of a (Woman) Writer*, Westport, Greenwood, 1988, pp. 293–301.

Furth, Isabella, 'Beee-e-een! Nation, Transformation and the Hyphen of Ethnicity in Kingston's *Tripmaster Monkey*', *MFS*, 40:1 (1994), 33–49.

Garner, Shirley Nelson, 'Breaking Silence: *The Woman Warrior*', in Diane P. Freedman, Olivia Frey and Frances Murphy Zauhar (eds), *The Intimate Critique: Autobiographical Literary Criticism*, Durham, NC, Duke University Press, 1993, pp. 117–125.

Giese, Julie, 'Comic Disruption in the Work of Maxine Hong Kingston', in Shannon Hengen and Nancy A. Walker (eds), *Performing Gender and Comedy: Theories, Texts and Contexts*, Amsterdam, Gordon and Breach, 1998, pp. 111–128.

Gilead, Sarah, 'Emigrant Selves: Narrative Strategies in Three Women's Autobiographies', *Criticism: A Quarterly for Literature and the Arts*, 30:1 (1988), 43–62.

Gilmore, Leiigh, *Autobiographies: A Feminist Theory of Women's Self-Representation*, Ithaca, Cornell University Press, 1994.

Goellnicht, Donald C., 'Father Land and/or Mother Tongue: The Divided Female Subject in Kogawa's *Obasan* and Hong Kingston's *The Woman Warrior*', in Janice Morgan, Colette T. Hall, Carol L. Snyder and Holly Mite (eds), *Redefining Autobiography in Twentieth-Century Women's Fiction: An Essay Collection*, New York, Garland, 1991, pp. 119–134.

——, 'Tang Ao in America: Male Subject Positions in *China Men*', in Shirley Geok-lin Lim and Amy Ling (eds), *Reading the Literatures of Asian America*, Philadelphia, Temple University Press, 1992, pp. 191–214.

Goldman, Marlene, 'Naming the Unspeakable: The Mapping of Female Identity in Maxine Hong Kingston's *The Woman Warrior*', in

Anne E. Brown and Marjanne E. Gooze (eds), *International Women's Writing: New Landscapes of Identity*, Westport, Greenwood, 1995, pp. 223–232.

Gotera, Vincente F., '"I've Never Read Anything Like It": Student Responses to *The Woman Warrior*', in Shirley Geok-lin Lim (ed.), *Approaches to Teaching Kingston's* The Woman Warrior, New York, Modern Language Association of America, 1991, pp. 64–73.

Grice, Helena, *Negotiating Identities: Asian Women's Writing*, Manchester, Manchester University Press, 2002.

Grobman, Laurie, 'Toward a Multicultural Pedagogy: Literary and Nonliterary Traditions', *MELUS*, 26:1 (2001), 221–240.

Hattori, Tomo, 'Psycholinguistic Orientalism in Criticism of *The Woman Warrior* and *Obasan*', in Sandra Kumamoto Stanley (ed.), *Other Sisterhoods: Literary Theory and U.S. Women of Color*, Urbana, University of Illinois Press, 1998, pp. 119–138.

——, '*China Man*, Autoeroticism and the Remains of Asian America', *Novel: A Forum on Fiction*, 31:2 (1998), 215–236.

Hayes, Daniel, 'Autobiography's Secret', *A/B: Auto/Biography Studies*, 12:2 (1997), 243–260.

Haynes, Rosetta R., 'Intersections of Race, Gender, Sexuality and Experimentation in the Autobiographical Writings of Cherríe Moraga and Maxine Hong Kingston', *Contributions in Women's Studies*, 189 (2001), 133–146. Reprinted in Diane Long Hoeveler and Janet K. Boles (eds), *Women of Color: Defining the Issues, Hearing the Voices*, Westport, Greenwood, 2001, pp. 133–145.

Henke, Suzette A., 'Women's Life-Writing and the Minority Voice: Maya Angelou, Maxine Hong Kingston, and Alice Walker', in Melvin J. Friedman and Ben Siegel (eds), *Traditions, Voices, and Dreams: The American Novel since the 1960s*, Newark, University of Delaware Press, 1995, pp. 210–233.

Ho, Wendy, 'Mother/Daughter Writing and the Politics of Race and Sex in Maxine Hong Kingston's *The Woman Warrior*', in Shirley Hune, Hyung-chan Kim, Stephen S. Fugita and Amy Ling (eds), *Asian Americans: Comparative and Global Perspectives*, Pullman, Washington State University Press, 1991, pp. 225–238.

Holaday, Woon-Ping Chin, 'From Ezra Pound to Maxine Hong Kingston: Expressions of Chinese Thought in American Literature', *MELUS*, 5:2 (1978), 15–24.

Homsher, Deborah, '*The Woman Warrior*, by Maxine Hong Kingston: A Bridging of Autobiography and Fiction', *Iowa Review*, 10:4 (1979), 93–98.

Horton, Karen, 'Honolulu Interview: Maxine Hong Kingston', in Paul Skenazy and Tera Martin (eds), *Conversations with Maxine Hong Kingston*, Jackson, University Press of Mississippi, 1998, pp. 5–13.

Hoy, Jody, 'To Be Able to See the Tao', in Paul Skenazy and Tera Martin (eds), *Conversations with Maxine Hong Kingston*, Jackson, University Press of Mississippi, 1998, pp. 47–66.

Huang, Guiyou, 'Maxine Hong Kingston (1940–)', in Emmanuel S. Nelson (ed.), *Asian American Novelists: A Bio-Bibliographical Critical Sourcebook*, Westport, Greenwood, 2000, pp. 138–155.

Huang, Hsin-ya, 'Three Women's Texts and the Healing Power of the Other Woman', *Concentric: Literary and Cultural Studies*, 28:1 (2003), 153–180.

Hunsaker, Steven V., 'Nation, Family, and Language in Victor Perera's *Rites* and Maxine Hong Kingston's *The Woman Warrior*', *Biography: An Interdisciplinary Quarterly*, 20:4 (1997), 437–461.

Hunt, Linda, '"I Could Not Figure Out What was My Village": Gender vs. Ethnicity in Maxine Hong Kingston's *The Woman Warrior*', *MELUS*, 12:3 (1985), 5–12.

Ishihara, Toshi, 'Meanings of Translation in Maxine Hong Kingston's *Tripmaster Monkey: His Fake Book*', *AALA Journal*, 2 (1995), 25–38.

Islas, Arturo, 'Maxine Hong Kingston', in Marilyn Yalom (ed.), *Women Writers of the West Coast: Speaking of Their Lives and Careers*, Santa Barbara, Capra, 1983, pp. 11–19.

—— and Marilyn Yalom, 'Interview with Maxine Hong Kingston', in Paul Skenazy and Tera Martin (eds), *Conversations with Maxine Hong Kingston*, Jackson, University Press of Mississippi, 1998, pp. 21–32.

Janette, Michele, 'The Angle We're Joined At: A Conversation with Maxine Hong Kingston', *Transition*, 71 (1996), 140–157.

Jenkins, Ruth Y., 'Authorizing Female Voice and Experience: Ghosts and Spirits in Kingston's *The Woman Warrior* and Allende's *The House of the Spirits*', *MELUS*, 19:3 (1994), 61–73.

Johnson, Sue Ann, 'Empowerment Through Mythological Imaginings in Woman Warrior', *Biography: An Interdisciplinary Quarterly*, 16:2 (1993), 136–146.

Juhasz, Suzanne, 'Towards a Theory of Form in Feminist Auto-biography: Kate Millet's *Flying and Sita*; Maxine Hong Kingston's *The Woman Warrior*', *International Journal of Women's Studies*, 2 (1979), 62–75.

——, 'Maxine Hong Kingston: Narrative Technique and Female Identity', in Catherine Rainwater and William J. Scheick (eds), *Contemporary American Women Writers: Narrative Strategies*, Lexington, University Press of Kentucky, 1985, pp. 173–189.

Kalogeras, Yiorgos, 'Producing History and Telling Stories: Maxine Hong Kingston's *China Men* and Zeese Papanikolas's *Buried Unsung*', in Amritjit Singh and Joseph T. Skerrett, Jr (eds), *Memory* and *Cultural Politics: New Approaches to American Ethnic Literatures*, Boston, Northeastern University Press, 1996, pp. 227–244.

Kang, Laura Hyun Yi, *Enfiguring Asian/American Women: Compositional Subjects*, Durham, Duke University Press, 2002.

Keenan, Sally, 'Crossing Boundaries: The Revisionary Writing of Maxine Hong Kingston', in Helena Grice (ed.), 'Asian American Literary Feminisms', Special Issue of *Hitting Critical Mass: A Journal of Asian American Cultural Criticism*, 6:2 (Spring 2000), 75–94.

Kehler, Dorothea, 'Shakespeare, Okada, Kingston: The First Generation', *Comparatist: Journal of the Southern Comparative Literature Association*, 22 (1998), 110–122.

Kennedy, Colleen, and Deborah Morse, 'A Dialogue with(in) Tradition: Two Perspectives on *The Woman Warrior*', in Shirley Geok-lin Lim (ed.), *Approaches to Teaching Kingston's* The Woman Warrior, New York, Modern Language Association of America, 1991, pp. 121–130.

Komenaka, April R., 'Autobiography as a Sociolinguistic Resource: Maxine Hong Kingston's *The Woman Warrior*', *International Journal of the Sociology of Language*, 69 (1988), 105–118.

Koss, Nicholas, '"Will the Real Wittman Ah Sing Please Stand Up": Cultural Identity in *Tripmaster Monkey: His Fake Book*', *Fu Jen Studies: Literature & Linguistics*, 26 (1993), 24–50.

Kubota, Gary, 'Maxine Hong Kingston: Something Comes Outside onto the Paper', in Paul Skenazy and Tera Martin (eds), *Conversations with Maxine Hong Kingston*, Jackson, University Press of Mississippi, 1998, pp. 1–4.

Kurian, Manju S., 'Negotiating Power from the Margins: Lessons from Years of Racial Memory', *Women and Language*, 19:1 (1996), 27–31.

Lan, Feng, 'The Female Individual and the Empire: A Historicist Approach to *Mulan* and Kingston's *Woman Warrior*', *Comparative Literature*, 55:3 (2003), 229–245.

Lappas, Catherine, '"The Way I Heard It Was...": Myth, Memory, and Autobiography in *Storyteller* and *The Woman Warrior*', *CEA Critic: An Official Journal of the College English Association*, 57:1 (1994), 57–67.

Lau, Joseph S. M., 'Kingston as Exorcist', in Michael S. Duke (ed.), *Modern Chinese Women Writers: Critical Appraisals*, Armonk, Sharpe (An East Gate Book), 1989, pp. 44–52.

Lee, Hsiu-chuan, 'Genre-Crossing: Kingston's *The Woman Warrior* and Its Discursive Community', *Paroles Gelees: UCLA French Studies*, 14:2 (1996), 87–102.

Lee, Katherine Hyunmi, 'The Poetics of Liminality and Misidentification: Winnifred Eaton's *Me* and Maxine Hong Kingston's *The Woman Warrior*', *Studies in the Literary Imagination*, 37:1 (2004), 17–33.

Lee, Ken-fan, 'Cultural Translation and the Exorcist: A Reading of Kingston's and Tan's Ghost Stories', *MELUS*, 29:2 (2004), 105–127.

Lee, Rachel, 'Claiming Land, Claiming Voice, Claiming Canon: Institutionalized Challenges in Kingston's *China Men* and *The Woman Warrior*', in Wendy L. Ng, Soo-young Chin, James S. Moy and Gary Y. Okihiro (eds), *Reviewing Asian America: Locating Diversity*, Pullman, Washington State University Press, 1995, pp. 147–159.

——, *The Americas of Asian American Literature: Gendered Fictions of Nation and Transnation*, Princeton: Princeton University Press, 1999.

Lee, Robert A., 'Ethnic Renaissance: Rudolfo Anaya, Louise Erdrich, and Maxine Hong Kingston', in Graham Clarke (ed.), *The New American Writing: Essays on American Literature Since 1970*, New York, St. Martin's, 1990, pp. 139–164.

Lee, Robert G., '*The Woman Warrior* as an Intervention in Asian American Historiography', in Shirley Geok-lin Lim (ed.), *Approaches to Teaching Kingston's* The Woman Warrior, New York, Modern Language Association of America, 1991, pp. 52–63.

Lee, Yoon Sun, 'Kingston's *China Men*: Circumscribing the Romance of Deterritorialization', *Yale Journal of Criticism: Interpretation in the Humanities*, 11:2 (1998), 465–484.

Li, David Leiwei, 'The Naming of a Chinese American "I": Cross-Cultural Sign/ifications in *The Woman Warrior*', *Criticism: A Quarterly for Literature and the Arts*, 30:4 (1988), 497–515.

——, '*China Men*: Maxine Hong Kingston and the American Canon', *American Literary History*, 2:3 (1990), 482–502.

——, 'The Production of Chinese American Tradition: Displacing American Orientalist Discourse', in Shirley Geok-lin Lim, Amy Ling and Elaine H. Kim (eds), *Reading the Literatures of Asian America*, Philadelphia, Temple University Press, 1992, pp. 319–332.

Li, Juan, 'Pidgin and Code-Switching: Linguistic Identity and Multicultural Consciousness in Maxine Hong Kingston's *Tripmaster Monkey*', *Language and Literature*, 13:3 (2004), 269–287.

Li, Zeng, 'Diasporic Self, Cultural Other: Negotiating Ethnicity through Transformation in the Fiction of Tan and Kingston', *Language and Literature*, 28 (2003), 1–15.

Lidoff, Joan, 'Autobiography in a Different Voice: Maxine Hong Kingston's *The Woman Warrior*', *A/B: Auto/Biography Studies*, 3:3 (1987), 29–35. Reprinted as 'Autobiography in a Different Voice: *The Woman Warrior* and the Question of Genre', in Shirley Geok-lin Lim (ed.), *Approaches to Teaching Kingston's* The Woman Warrior, New York, Modern Language Association of America, 1991, pp. 116–120.

Lim, Shirley Geok-lin, 'The Tradition of Chinese American Women's Life Stories: Thematics of Race and Gender in Jade Snow Wong's *Fifth Chinese Daughter* and Maxine Hong Kingston's *The Woman Warrior*', in Margo Culley (ed.), *American Women's Autobiography: Fea(s)ts of Memory*, Madison, University of Wisconsin Press, 1992, pp. 252–267.

—, 'Feminist and Ethnic Literary Theories in Asian American Literature', *Feminist Studies*, 19:3 (Autumn, 1993), 571–595.

—, '"Growing with Stories": Chinese American Identities, Textual Identities (Maxine Hong Kingston)', in John R. Maitino and David R. Peck (eds), *Teaching American Ethnic Literatures: Nineteen Essays*, Albuquerque, University of New Mexico Press, 1996, pp. 273–291.

— and Amy Ling (eds), *Reading the Literatures of Asian America*, Philadelphia, Temple University Press, 1992.

Lin, Patricia, 'Use of Media and Other Resources to Situate *The Woman Warrior*', in Shirley Geok-lin Lim (ed.), *Approaches to Teaching Kingston's* The Woman Warrior, New York, Modern Language Association of America, 1991, pp. 37–43.

—, 'Clashing Constructs of Reality: Reading Maxine Hong Kingston's *Tripmaster Monkey: His Fakebook* as Indigenous Ethnography', in Shirley Geok-lin Lim, Amy Ling and Elaine H. Kim (eds), *Reading the Literatures of Asian America*, Philadelphia, Temple University Press, 1992, pp. 333–348.

Ling, Amy, 'Thematic Threads in Maxine Hong Kingston's *The Woman Warrior*', *Tamkang Review: A Quarterly of Comparative Studies between Chinese and Foreign Literatures*, 14:1–4 (1983–1984), 155–164.

—, *Between Worlds: Women Writers of Chinese Ancestry*, New York, Pergamon, 1990.

—, 'Maxine Hong Kingston and the Dialogic Dilemma of Asian American Writers', *Bucknell Review: A Scholarly Journal of Letters, Arts and Sciences*, 39:1 (1995), 151–166.

—, 'Chinese American Women Writers: The Tradition behind Maxine Hong Kingston', in A. LaVonne Brown Ruoff and Jerry W. Ward (eds), *Redefining American Literary History*, New York, Modern Language Association of America, 1990, pp. 219–236. Reprinted in Sau-ling Cynthia Wong (ed.), *Maxine Hong Kingston's* The Woman Warrior: *A Casebook*, New York, Oxford University Press, 1999, pp. 135–158.

Ling, Jinqi, 'Identity Crisis and Gender Politics: Reappropriating Asian American Masculinity', in King-kok Cheung (ed), *An Interethnic Companion to Asian American Literature*, Cambridge, Cambridge University Press, 1997, pp. 312–337.

Linton, Patricia, '"What Stories the Wind Would Tell": Representation and Appropriation in Maxine Hong Kingston's *China Men*', *MELUS*, 19:4 (1994), 37–48.

Lionnet, Françoise, *Postcolonial Representations: Women, Literature, Identity*, Ithaca, Cornell University Press, 1995.

Liu, Kate, 'National History Re-Visioned and Hybridized: Assimilation and the American Dream in Kingston's *China Men*', *Fu Jen Studies: Literature & Linguistics*, 26 (1993), 1–23.

Lowe, John, 'Monkey Kings and Mojo: Postmodern Ethnic Humor in Kingston, Reed, and Vizenor', *MELUS*, 21:4 (1996), 103–126.

Lowe, Lisa, *Immigrant Acts: On Asian American Cultural Politics*, Durham, Duke University Press, 1996.

Ludwig, Sami, '"You Can See Behind You Like a Bat": Metaphorical Constructions and Intercultural Understanding in Maxine Hong Kingston's *The Woman Warrior*', *Hitting Critical Mass: A Journal of Asian American Cultural Criticism*, 4:1 (1996), 81–102.

——, 'Cultural Identity as "Spouse": Limitations and Possibilities of a Metaphor in Maxine Hong Kingston's *The Woman Warrior* and Bharati Mukherjee's *Jasmine*', in Peter O. Stummer and Christopher Balme (eds), *Fusion of Cultures?*, Amsterdam, Rodopi, 1996, pp. 103–110.

McBride, Paul W., '*The Woman Warrior* in the History Classroom', in Shirley Geok-lin Lim (ed.), *Approaches to Teaching Kingston's The Woman Warrior*, New York, Modern Language Association of America, 1991, pp. 93–100.

Madsen, Deborah L., '(Dis)Figuration: The Body as Icon in the Writings of Maxine Hong Kingston', *Yearbook of English Studies*, 24 (1994), 237–250.

——, *Maxine Hong Kingston*, Farmington Hills, Michigan, Gale, 2001.

Maini, Irma, 'Writing the Asian American Artist: Maxine Hong Kingston's *Tripmaster Monkey: His Fake Book*', *MELUS*, 25:3–4 (2000), 243–264.

Mandelbaum, Paul, 'Rising From the Ashes: A Profile of Maxine Hong Kingston', *Poets & Writers*, 26:3 (1st May, 1998), 46.

Maxey, Ruth, '"The East is Where Things Begin": Writing the Ancestral Homeland in Amy Tan and Maxine Hong Kingston', *Orbis Litterarum*, 60:1 (2005), 1–15.

Melchior, Bonnie, 'A Marginal "I": The Autobiographical Self Deconstructed in Maxine Hong Kingston's *The Woman Warrior*', *Biography: An Interdisciplinary Quarterly*, 17:3 (1994), 281–295.

Melton, Judith M., '*The Woman Warrior* in the Women's Classroom', in Shirley Geok-lin Lim (ed.), *Approaches to Teaching Kingston's The Woman Warrior*, New York, Modern Language Association of America, 1991, pp. 74–79.

Miller, Elise, 'Kingston's *The Woman Warrior*: The Object of Autobiographical Relations', in Vera J. Camden (ed.), *Compromise Formations: Current Directions in Psychoanalytic Criticism*, Kent, Kent State University, 1989, pp. 138–154.

Miller, Lucien, and Hui-chuan Chang, 'Fiction and Autobiography: Spatial Form in *The Golden Cangue* and *The Woman Warrior*', *Tamkang Review: A Quarterly of Comparative Studies between Chinese and Foreign Literatures*, 15:1–4 (1984–1985), 75–96. Reprinted in Michael S. Duke (ed.), *Modern Chinese Women Writers: Critical Appraisals*, Armonk, Sharpe (An East Gate Book), 1989, pp. 25–43.

Miller, Margaret, 'Threads of Identity in Maxine Hong Kingston's *Woman Warrior*', *Biography: An Interdisciplinary Quarterly*, 6:1 (1983), 13–33.

Mitchell, Carol, '"Talking Story" in *The Woman Warrior*: An Analysis of the Use of Folklore', *Kentucky Folklore Record: A Regional Journal of Folklore and Folklife*, 27:1–2 (1981), 5–12.

Monsma, Bradley John, '"Active Readers … Obverse Tricksters": Trickster-Texts and Cross-Cultural Reading', *Modern Language Studies*, 26:4 (1996), 83–98.

Morante, Linda, 'From Silence to Song: The Triumph of Maxine Hong Kingston', *Frontiers: A Journal of Women Studies*, 9:2 (1987), 78–82.

Myers, Victoria, 'The Significant Fictivity of Maxine Hong Kingston's *The Woman Warrior*', *Biography: An Interdisciplinary Quarterly*, 9:2 (1986), 112–125.

——, 'Speech-Act Theory and Search for Identity in *The Woman Warrior*', in Shirley Geok-lin Lim (ed.), *Approaches to Teaching Kingston's* The Woman Warrior, New York, Modern Language Association of America, 1991, pp. 131–137.

Mylan, Sheryl A., 'The Mother as Other: Orientalism in Maxine Hong Kingston's *The Woman Warrior*', in Elizabeth Brown-Guillory (ed.), *Women of Color: Mother–Daughter Relationships in 20th-Century Literature*, Austin, University of Texas Press, 1996, pp. 132–152.

Neubauer, Carol E., 'Developing Ties to the Past: Photography and Other Sources of Information in Maxine Hong Kingston's *China Men*', *MELUS*, 10:4 (1983), 17–36.

Nishime, LeiLani, 'Engendering Genre: Gender and Nationalism in *China Men* and *The Woman Warrior*', *MELUS*, 20:1 (1995), 67–82.

Ordonez, Elizabeth J., 'Narrative Texts by Ethnic Women: Rereading the Past, Reshaping the Future', *MELUS*, 9:3 (1982), 19–28.

Outka, Paul, 'Publish or Perish: Food, Hunger, and Self-Construction in Maxine Hong Kingston's *The Woman Warrior*', *Contemporary Literature*, 38:3 (1997), 447–482.

Perry, Donna, 'Maxine Hong Kingston', in Donna Perry (ed.), *Backtalk: Women Writers Speak Out*, New Brunswick, Rutgers University Press, 1993, pp. 171–193. Reprinted in Paul Skenazy and Tera Martin (eds), *Conversations with Maxine Hong Kingston*, Jackson, University Press of Mississippi, 1998, pp. 168–188.

Peterson, Marilyn, and Deirdre Lashgari, 'Teaching *The Woman Warrior* to High School and Community College Students', in Shirley Geok-lin Lim (ed.), *Approaches to Teaching Kingston's* The Woman Warrior, New York, Modern Language Association of America, 1991, pp. 101–107.

Petit, Angela, '"Words So Strong": Maxine Hong Kingston's "No Name Woman" Introduces Students to the Power of Words', *Journal of Adolescent and Adult Literacy*, 46:6 (2003), 482–490.

Pfaff, Timothy, 'Talk with Mrs. Kingston', in Paul Skenazy and Tera Martin (eds), *Conversations with Maxine Hong Kingston*, Jackson, University Press of Mississippi, 1998, pp. 14–20.

Quinby, Lee, 'The Subject of Memoirs: The Woman Warrior's Technology of Ideographic Selfhood', in Sidonie Smith and Julia Watson (eds), *De/Colonizing the Subject: The Politics of Gender in Women's Autobiography*, Minneapolis, University of Minnesota Press, 1992, pp. 297–320.

Rabine, Leslie W., 'No Lost Paradise: Social Gender and Symbolic Gender in the Writings of Maxine Hong Kingston', *Signs: Journal of Women in Culture and Society*, 12:3 (1987), 471–492. Reprinted in Sau-ling Cynthia Wong (ed.), *Maxine Hong Kingston's* The Woman Warrior: *A Casebook*, New York, Oxford University Press, 1999, pp. 85–109.

Rabinowitz, Paula, 'Naming, Magic, and Documentary: The Subversion of the Narrative in *Song of Solomon*, *Ceremony*, and *China Men*', in Vivian Patraka and Louise A. Tilly (eds), *Feminist Re-Visions: What Has Been and Might Be*, Ann Arbor, Women's Studies Program, University of Michigan, 1983, pp. 26–42.

——, 'Eccentric Memories: A Conversation with Maxine Hong Kingston', *Michigan Quarterly Review*, 26:1 (1987), 177–187. Reprinted in Paul Skenazy and Tera Martin (eds), *Conversations with Maxine Hong Kingston*, Jackson, University Press of Mississippi, 1998, pp. 67–76.

Rose, Shirley K., 'Metaphors and Myths of Cross-Cultural Literacy: Autobiographical Narratives by Maxine Hong Kingston, Richard Rodriguez, and Malcolm X', *MELUS*, 14:1 (1987), 3–15.

Royal, Derek Parker, 'Literary Genre as Ethnic Resistance in Maxine Hong Kingston's *Tripmaster Monkey: His Fake Book*', *MELUS*, 29:2 (2004), 141–156.

Rusk, Lauren, 'Voicing the Harmonic Self: Maxine Hong Kingston's *The Woman Warrior*', *Constructions*, 9 (1994), 13–30.

——, 'The Collective Self: Maxine Hong Kingston and Virginia Woolf', in Laura Davis, Jeanette McVicker and Jeanne Dubino (eds), *Virginia Woolf and Her Influences: Selected Papers from the Seventh Annual Conference on Virginia Woolf*, New York, Pace University Press, 1998, pp. 181–186.

——, *The Life Writing of Otherness: Woolf, Baldwin, Kingston, and Winterson*, New York, Routledge, 2002.

San Juan, E., Jr., 'Beyond Identity Politics: The Predicament of the Asian Writer in Late Capitalism', *American Literary History*, 3:3 (1991), 542–565.

Sato, Gayle K. Fujita, '*The Woman Warrior* as a Search for Ghosts', in Shirley Geok-lin Lim (ed.), *Approaches to Teaching Kingston's* The Woman Warrior, New York, Modern Language Association of America, 1991, pp. 138–145.

——, 'Ghosts as Chinese-American Constructs in Maxine Hong Kingston's *The Woman Warrior*', in Lynette Carpenter and Wendy K. Kolmar (eds), *Haunting the House of Fiction: Feminist Perspectives on Ghost Stories by American Women*, Knoxville, University of Tennessee Press, 1991, pp. 193–214.

Schmidt, Jan Zlotnik, 'The Other: A Study of the Persona in Several Contemporary Women's Autobiographies', *CEA Critic: An Official Journal of the College English Association*, 43:1 (1980), 24–31.

Schroeder, Eric James, '"As Truthful as Possible": An Interview with Maxine Hong Kingston', *Writing on the Edge*, 7:2 (1996), 83–96. Reprinted in Paul Skenazy and Tera Martin (eds), *Conversations with Maxine Hong Kingston*, Jackson, University Press of Mississippi, 1998, pp. 215–228.

Schueller, Malini Johar, 'Theorizing Ethnicity and Subjectivity: Maxine Hong Kingston's *Tripmaster Monkey* and Amy Tan's *The Joy Luck Club*', *Genders*, 15 (1992), 72–85.

—— 'Questioning Race and Gender Definitions: Dialogic Subversions in *The Woman Warrior*', *Criticism: A Quarterly for Literature and the Arts*, 31:4 (1989), 421–437. Reprinted in Lois Parkinson Zamora (ed.), *Contemporary American Women Writers: Gender, Class, Ethnicity*, London, Longman, 1998, pp. 51–66.

Seshachari, Neila C., 'An Interview with Maxine Hong Kingston', *Weber Studies: An Interdisciplinary Humanities Journal*, 12:1 (1995), 7–26.

——, 'Reinventing Peace: Conversations with Tripmaster Maxine Hong Kingston', in Paul Skenazy and Tera Martin (eds), *Conversations with Maxine Hong Kingston*, Jackson, University Press of Mississippi, 1998, pp. 192–214.

Shan, Te-hsing, 'Law as Literature, Literature as Law: Articulating "The Laws" in Maxine Hong Kingston's *China Men*', *Tamkang*

Review: A Quarterly of Comparative Studies between Chinese and Foreign Literatures, 26:1–2 (1995), 235–264.

Shapiro, Elliott H., 'Authentic Watermelon: Maxine Hong Kingston's American Novel', *MELUS*, 26:1 (2001), 5–28.

Shih, Shu-mei, 'Exile and Intertextuality in Maxine Hong Kingston's *China Men*', in James Whitlark and Wendell Aycock (eds), *The Literature of Emigration and Exile*, Lubbock, Texas Tech University Press, 1992, pp. 65–77.

Shostak, Debra, 'Maxine Hong Kingston's Fake Books', in Amritjit Singh, Joseph T. Skerrett and Robert E. Hogan (eds), *Memory, Narrative, and Identity: New Essays in Ethnic American Literatures*, Boston, Northeastern University Press, 1994, pp. 233–260.

Simmons, Diane, 'Maxine Hong Kingston's *Woman Warrior* and *Shaman*: Fighting Women in the New World', *FEMSPEC*, 2:1 (2000), 49–65.

Skandera-Trombley, Laura E. (ed.), *Critical Essays on Maxine Hong Kingston*, New York, G. K. Hall, 1998.

Skenazy, Paul, 'Replayingtime', *Enclitic*, 11:3 (23) (1989), 36–42.

——, 'Kingston at the University', in Paul Skenazy and Tera Martin (eds), *Conversations with Maxine Hong Kingston*, Jackson, University Press of Mississippi, 1998, pp. 118–158.

——, 'Coming Home', in Paul Skenazy and Tera Martin (eds), *Conversations with Maxine Hong Kingston*, Jackson, University Press of Mississippi, 1998, pp. 104–117.

Sledge, Linda Ching, 'Maxine Kingston's *China Men*: The Family Historian as Epic Poet', *MELUS*, 7:4 (1980), 3–22.

——, 'Oral Tradition in Kingston's *China Men*', in A. LaVonne Brown Ruoff and Jerry W. Ward (eds), *Redefining American Literary History*, New York, Modern Language Association of America, 1990, pp. 142–154.

Smith, Jeanne R., 'Rethinking American Culture: Maxine Hong Kingston's Cross-Cultural *Tripmaster Monkey*', *Modern Language Studies*, 26:4 (1996), 71–81.

Smith, Joan, 'Creating Peace Out of Pathos', in Paul Skenazy and Tera Martin (eds), *Conversations with Maxine Hong Kingston*, Jackson, University Press of Mississippi, 1998, pp. 189–191.

Smith, Sidonie, *A Poetics of Women's Autobiography: Marginality and the Fictions of Self-Representation*, Bloomington, Indiana University Press, 1987.

——, *Subjectivity, Identity, and the Body: Women's Autobiographical Practices in the Twentieth Century*, Bloomington, Indiana University press, 1993.

——, Maxine Hong Kingston's *Woman Warrior*: Filiality and Woman's Autobiographical Storytelling', in Robyn R. Warhol and

Diane Price Herndl (eds), *Feminisms: An Anthology of Literary Theory and Criticism*, New Brunswick, Rutgers University Press, 1997, pp. 1117–1137. Reprinted in Sau-ling Cynthia Wong (ed.), *Maxine Hong Kingston's* The Woman Warrior: *A Casebook*, New York, Oxford University Press, 1999, pp. 57–83.

Suzuki-Martinez, Sharon, 'Trickster Strategies: Challenging American Identity, Community, and Art in Kingston's *Tripmaster Monkey*', in Wendy L. Ng, Soo-young Chin, James S. Moy and Gary Y. Okihiro (eds), *Reviewing Asian America: Locating Diversity*, Pullman, Washington State University Press, 1995, pp. 161–170.

Tanner, James T. F., 'Walt Whitman's Presence in Maxine Hong Kingston's *Tripmaster Monkey: His Fake Book*', *MELUS*, 20:4 (1995), 61–74.

Thomas, Brook, '*China Men*, United States v. Wong Kim Ark, and the Question of Citizenship', *American Quarterly*, 50:4 (1998), 689–717.

Thompson, Phyllis Hoge, 'This Is the Story I Heard: A Conversation with Maxine Hong Kingston and Earl Kingston', *Biography: An Interdisciplinary Quarterly*, 6:1 (1983), 1–12.

TuSmith, Bonnie, 'Literary Tricksterism: Maxine Hong Kingston's *The Woman Warrior: Memoirs of a Girlhood among Ghosts*', *Lit: Literature Interpretation Theory*, 2:4 (1991), 249–259. Reprinted in Carol J. Singley and Susan Elizabeth Sweeney (eds), *Anxious Power: Reading, Writing, and Ambivalence in Narrative by Women*, Albany, SUNY Press, 1993, pp. 279–294.

——, *All My Relatives: Commuunity in Contemporary Ethnic American Literatures*, Ann Arbor, University of Michigan Press, 1993.

Tyler, Anne, 'Manic Monologue', *New Republic*, 200 (17 April, 1989), 44–46.

VanSpanckeren, Kathryn, 'The Asian Literary Background of *The Woman Warrior*', in Shirley Geok-lin Lim (ed.), *Approaches to Teaching Kingston's* The Woman Warrior, New York, Modern Language Association of America, 1991, pp. 44–51.

Vizenor, Gerald, 'Postmodern Monkey', *American Book Review*, 11:6 (1990), 17.

Wang, Alfred S., 'Maxine Hong Kingston's Reclaiming of America: The Birthright of the Chinese-American Male', *South Dakota Review*, 26:1 (1988), 18–29.

——, 'Lu Hsun and Maxine Hong Kingston: Medicine as a Symbol in Chinese and Chinese American Literature', *Literature and Medicine*, 8 (1989), 1–21.

Wang, Jennie, '*Tripmaster Monkey*: Kingston's Postmodern Representation of a New "China Man"', *MELUS*, 20:1 (1995), 101–114.

——, 'The Myth of Kingston's "No Name Woman": Making Contextual and Intertextual Connections in Teaching Asian American

Literature', *CEA Critic: An Official Journal of the College English Association*, 59:1 (1996), 21–32.

——, 'Reinterpreting Kingston's Feminist Agenda', in Luísa Maria Flora, Teresa F. A. Alves, and Teresa Cid (eds), *Feminine Identities*, Lisbon, Colibri, 2002, pp. 205–226.

Wang, Qun, '"Double Consciousness", Sociological Imagination, and the Asian American Experience', *Race, Gender & Class: Asian American Voices*, 4:3 (1997), 88–94.

Wang, Veronica, 'Reality and Fantasy: The Chinese-American Woman's Quest for Identity', *MELUS*, 12:3 (1985), 23–31.

Wang, Veronica C., 'In Search of Self: The Dislocated Female Émigré Wanderer in Chuang Hua's Crossings', in Barbara Frey Waxman (ed.), *Multicultural Literatures through Feminist/Poststructuralist Lenses*, Knoxville, University of Tennessee Press, 1993, pp. 22–36.

Waxman, Barbara Frey, 'Feeding the "Hunger of Memory" and an Appetite for the Future: The Ethnic "Storied" Self and the American Authored Self in Ethnic Autobiography', in John C. Hawley (ed.), *Cross-Addressing: Resistance Literature and Cultural Borders*, Albany, SUNY Press, 1996, pp. 207–219.

Weldy, Lance, 'The Rhetoric of Intertextuality: Maxine Hong Kingston's Emasculation of *China Men* through Li Ruzhen's *Flowers in the Mirror*', *Language and Literature*, 28 (2003), 27–42.

Wilcoxon, Hardy C., 'No Types of Ambiguity: Teaching Chinese American Texts in Hong Kong', in William E. Cain and Julia Brown (eds), *Ethnicity and the American Short Story*, New York, Garland, 1997, pp. 141–154.

Williams, A. Noelle, 'Parody and Pacifist Transformations in Maxine Hong Kingston's *Tripmaster Monkey: His Fake Book*', *MELUS*, 20:1 (1995), 83–100.

Wong, Sau-ling Cynthia, 'Necessity and Extravagance in Maxine Hong Kingston's *The Woman Warrior*: Art and the Ethnic Experience', *MELUS*, 15:1 (1988), 4–26.

——, 'Kingston's Handling of Traditional Chinese Sources', in Shirley Geok-lin Lim (ed.), *Approaches to Teaching Kingston's* The Woman Warrior, New York, Modern Language Association of America, 1991, pp. 26–36.

——, 'Autobiography as Guided Chinatown Tour? Maxine Hong Kingston's *The Woman Warrior* and the Chinese-American Autobiographical Controversy', in James Robert Payne (ed.), *Multicultural Autobiography: American Lives*, Knoxville, University of Tennessee Press, 1992, pp. 248–279. Reprinted in Sau-ling Cynthia Wong (ed.), *Maxine Hong Kingston's* The Woman Warrior: A Casebook, New York, Oxford University Press, 1999, pp. 29–53.

Woo, Deborah, 'Maxine Hong Kingston: The Ethnic Writer and the

Burden of Dual Authenticity', *Amerasia Journal*, 16:1 (1990), 173–200.

Woo, Eunjoo, '"The Beginning Is Hers, the Ending, Mine": Chinese American Mother/Daughter Conflict and Reconciliation in Maxine Hong Kingston's *The Woman Warrior*', *Studies in Modern Fiction*, 9:1 (2002), 297–314.

Wu, Qing-yun, 'A Chinese Reader's Response to Maxine Hong Kingston's *China Men*', *MELUS*, 17:3 (1991–1992), 85–94.

Xiaojing, Zhou, 'Becoming Americans: Gish Jen's Typical American', in Katherine B. Payant and Toby Rose (eds), *The Immigrant Experience in North American Literature: Carving Out a Niche*, Westport, Greenwood, 1999, pp. 151–613.

Yalom, Marilyn, '*The Woman Warrior* as Postmodern Autobiography', in Shirley Geok-lin Lim (ed.), *Approaches to Teaching Kingston's* The Woman Warrior, New York, Modern Language Association of America, 1991, pp. 108–115.

Yu, Ning, 'A Strategy against Marginalization: The "High" and "Low" Cultures in Kingston's *China Men*', *College Literature*, 23:3 (1996), 73–87.

Yuan, Yuan, 'The Semiotics of China Narratives in the Con/Texts of Kingston and Tan', *Critique*, 40:3 (1999), 292–303.

Zhang, Ya-jie, 'A Chinese Woman's Response to Maxine Hong Kingston's *The Woman Warrior*', in Sau-ling Cynthia Wong (ed.), *Maxine Hong Kingston's* The Woman Warrior: *A Casebook*, New York, Oxford University Press, 1999, 17–21.

Index